The Art of Jewish Living
סדר חנכה Hanukkah

The Art of Jewish Living

סדר חנכה Hanukkah

by Dr. Ron Wolfson

Edited by Joel Lurie Grishaver

A project of
The Federation of Jewish Men's Clubs
and
The University of Judaism

The Federation of Jewish Men's Clubs, an arm of the Conservative
Movement, trains lay leadership and promotes Jewish education in
the home and synagogue.

The University of Judaism is an academic institution dedicated to the
study and enhancement of Jewish life.

Jules Porter Photographers, a leading photography studio in Los
Angeles, provided all photographic services for
The Art of Jewish Living: Hanukkah.

Alef Type and Design provided all typesetting and design services for
the Art of Jewish Living series.

Chart from page 80 from *Together: A Child-Parent Kit*, Issue Four by
Vicky Kelman. Reprinted by permission of The Melton Research
Center of The Jewish Theological Seminary of America, 3080
Broadway, New York, New York 10027. Copyright ©1984, 1990

ISBN NUMBER: 0-935665-25-0

Manufactured in the United States of America.

For

Havi Michele   Michael Louis

You are a great miracle to me.

CONTENTS

PREFACE

Dr. Ron Wolfson is an extraordinary family educator. As exemplified in his book, he knows that his target is not the registered student body of a school, but the intergenerational "mishpochah." His venue is not the school classroom with its chalk and blackboard, but the home with its kitchen, dining and living rooms. The tables, chairs and art of the home are not the clip-boards, bulletin boards and texts of the classroom. A home is not a classroom and its celebrations are not structured lesson plans.

While the family teaches and learns, parents are not instructors nor children students in the manner that school faculty and students are. The smells of our homes are not those of our school corridors; the paintings on our walls are not school posters. At home our children do not raise their hands to ask a question or sit in rows. The school practices and rehearses celebrations, but the home lives them.

All of this calls for a different way of transmitting Jewish information, values and attitudes. Family education calls for the empowerment of the family, which in our time has lost many of its talents.

Ron Wolfson's book understands the family and its multiple needs. It is written out of the situations and experiences of living families who come from all kinds of backgrounds. It is written by, for and of the Jewish family and enjoys a fine ear for its conversations, doubts and yearnings. A glance at the table of contents, from storytelling and recipes to theology, offers evidence of the author's comprehensive grasp of the family. The book is helpful to the family that strives to induct its members into the spirituality and joys of Jewishness and Judaism.

The Hebrew word *nes* is commonly translated as "miracle." In its original Jewish meaning, *nes* means "sign," from which the term "significant" is derived. Wolfson's Hanukkah book is a significant text in the neglected art of Jewish family education.

Harold M. Schulweis

FOREWORD

I will never forget the Maccabees of Omaha. As a boy, when I looked into the candles, I saw myself dressed in high rubber boots with too many buckles, armed with wet woolen mittens clipped on to my jacket, and protected by a muffler covering my face like a mask. There I was, strong, proud, Jewish, and ready to fight the wars of ice and snow to free the holy Temple. Somewhere, far in the background, Bing Crosby and Mel Torme were singing. In those blinks of an eye, Judah and I stood side-by-side, packing the slushballs tightly till they were solid ice. We whipped our ice balls, stormed the ice walls of the Syrian-Greek fortress, ambushed Syrian-Greek patrols in the alley—and in all ways were brave and courageous.

It was a time when Hanukkah really worked. It was family and lights, parties and presents, food and freedom, history and celebration. In those days, Hanukkah was easy and offered direct access to Jewish pride. Today, when my children light our Hanukkah lights in Southern California and their glow reflects onto the green lawn, I still look through the flames into frosted windows, steamed over by the heat, masking the Nebraska snowscape. I had a wonderful Jewish boyhood. Despite the snow, my Hanukkah memories are all warm and positive. They really were good times. Still, when Thanksgiving is over and the winter holiday season approaches, I am haunted by the ghost of Christmas past.

DEEP-FRIED HANUKKAH

My earliest Jewish memories are of celebrating Hanukkah during the cold evenings of a Midwestern winter. Our fireplace mantle became the center of life for eight days. On it, my parents placed a small green Hanukkah menorah—in those days "*ḥanukkiyah*" was something only Hebrew school teachers said. Next to it was the ubiquitous box of brightly colored candles. Above it was tacked a blue and silver banner that spelled "Happy Chanukah," each of the letters hinged to allow for folding. On the floor there was a stack of presents. To be more precise, the presents for that particular night.

My parents subscribed to the "one for each night" theory of Hanukkah gift-giving. The other presents were stashed away somewhere in the house. Each year my brothers and I surreptitiously searched for these hidden treasures both before and during the holiday.

The first and last nights of Hanukkah were always the best. They were the nights for "big" presents. The parental theory was, I guess, to start the week off with a bang and then keep the enthusiasm from dying. When I was five, the big present was a cowboy outfit, complete with a ten-gallon hat, fringed leather vest, chaps, plastic spurs, and best of all a pair of six-guns, complete with spangled holsters. Boy, did I love that outfit!

Of course, presents were not distributed until after the candlelighting ritual took place. We knew to begin the holiday with lighting the *shamash*, the servant candle, and the first night's candle, adding "one for each night" for the next seven nights. The biggest decision was which colors to use. The candles came in an array of bright colors and each of us boys had our favorites. Mine was blue. The greatest challenge was to get the small candles to stand up straight in the holders of the menorah. Usually, we melted a little wax off the bottom of the candle to make it stick. Finally, we would light the wicks and join in the blessings, after which we mumbled the Hebrew words to *Maoz Tzur*, Rock of Ages. The instant the last note was sung, the sounds of ripping wrapping paper filled the air.

The first night of Hanukkah also meant potato latkes. These Hanukkah pancakes, deep-fried in oil, were just about the best thing this side of french fries. What a project making latkes was! First the potatoes had to be peeled, then soaked in water. And in those days before food processors, the raw potatoes were cut into little cubes and, with great risk to the knuckles, hand-grated on a silver-colored device that reduced the potato to a mushy consistency which looked positively awful. Flour and grated onions were added. A proper sized dollop of the mixture was carefully lowered into a pan filled with crackling oil so we wouldn't be burned too badly by the splattering liquid. A quick frying of the pancake and then it was removed to a paper towel to soak up the excess grease. Of course, with three boys and a dad, my mother spent most of the first Hanukkah dinner churning out those latkes. Depending on whether the meal was *fleishig* or *milchig* (meat or dairy), we ate them with applesauce or sour cream. As with the *gribenes* of Passover, what these latkes did to my arteries, I do not want to know.

From dinner, we returned to our presents for general playing and rough-housing. Sometimes, we would play dreidle, the gambling game that employs the four-sided top. We would wager tiny gold-wrapped chocolate coins, Hanukkah gelt, from our gold net bags. Bedtime would come soon, and we would fall asleep dreaming of tomorrow's candles and presents.

THE GHOST OF CHRISTMAS PAST

December in Omaha was the height of the Christmas season. There was not a place you could go that didn't announce the fact that Christmas was coming. From the daily countdown in the newspaper of "shopping days 'til Christmas" to the incessant commercials on television, the holiday was everywhere. Our block became a virtual wonderland of sparkling lights outlining homes and trees, the stores and malls featured Christmas displays and merchandise—even our public school was adorned with a huge Christmas tree in the front entrance. The strains of the haunting Christmas music—from "Silent Night" to "The Little Drummer Boy" —filled the air. There was no escape.

To a little Jewish child, December was the first test of one's identity, the first realization that you were not like almost everybody else. How do you cope? What do you say to the clerk who wishes you a "Merry Christmas!?" How do you play Jesus in the annual school Christmas pageant? What can you possibly do to stop yourself from humming "I'm Dreaming of a White Christmas?"

My mother thought she had the answer. She would outdo Christmas. This explains the decorations, the presents each and every night, the piles of latkes, the Hanukkah gelt. It seemed to work, especially when our Christian next-door neighbor, Mrs. Lamm, called to complain to my mother that I had been teasing her son Alan: "You only have Christmas for one day; we have Hanukkah for eight!"

The plan worked marvelously until, one year, the fifth night of Hanukkah coincided with Christmas Eve, a fact of which I had been well aware. After the lights had been lit, the presents given, and the latkes consumed, my mother confidently tucked me into bed, saying:

"Well, Ronnie, wasn't Hanukkah wonderful tonight?"

"Yes, Mommy," I dutifully replied. "Mommy?"

"Yes, honey."

"Mommy, can we take down the Hanukkah things—just for tonight—so Santa Claus won't know we're Jewish?"

A plea for more presents? A rejection of my nascent Jewish identity? I think not. Looking back on it now, I believe it was a half-hearted wish not to be different, if just for one night.

As I grew older, the Hanukkah/Christmas dilemma presented new challenges. On the one hand, my exposure to Christmas increased. With my family in the grocery business, the Christmas season was the busiest of the year. In fact, the entire front parking lot of Louis Market was transformed into a giant Christmas tree lot. Once Christmas vacation began, I was pressed into service as a tree salesman. I am one of the few Jewish educators I know who can tell the difference between a Northwest pine and a Douglas fir, estimate the height of a tree within several inches by sight, and offer three tips on how to keep a Christmas tree fresh for several weeks.

School presented a whole set of problems. Hanukkah was barely, if ever, mentioned. And when it was, it was usually me who was chosen to tell the class about Hanukkah customs. These little opportunities elicited conflicting feelings of pride in sharing my heritage and yet, reinforced the undeniable fact that I was different.

My ambivalence about the season as a child turned to activism as an adolescent. As a leader in United Synagogue Youth, I found my confusion turned to anger as I fought for the elimination of Christmas from public school celebrations. One of the most painful battlegrounds was one of my favorite activities—singing. As an officer of the A Cappella Choir at Central High School, I argued with the choir director about the inclusion of Christian religious music in the Winter Concert. I lost, and joined my Jewish friends in a coping strategy that enabled us to stay in the choir, but not betray our religious beliefs.

When we came to a passage such as "Jesus, priceless treasure," we simply mouthed the words, pretending to sing.

As I reflect on my December dilemma experiences while growing up, I realize that Christmas was an important influence in my developing self-definition as a Jew. From the difficulty of understanding that Christmas was something I couldn't have, to the shaping of my identity as being different from most other people, to the assertion during my high school years that being different was something to be proud of, it is clear that Christmas heightens the awareness of one's Jewishness almost as much as any single Jewish holiday.

I began to see this little irony of Jewish life even more clearly as my wife Susie and I and our children confronted the winter season. Of course, many things have changed over the past thirty years. Hanukkah has been transformed from a "minor" holiday to a major celebration among Jews. Clearly, this development can be traced directly to the influence of Christmas and its commercialization. In the 1950's, my mother bought one or two Hanukkah decorations in the synagogue gift shop. In the 1980's, we shopped for Hanukkah supplies in the local drug store. And like my parents a generation earlier, we did our best to fill our home with Hanukkah celebration that was traditional and festive.

Nevertheless, despite living in a predominantly Jewish neighborhood and sending our children to Jewish day schools, our family had to confront the dominant culture as Christmas took over the television, the shopping malls, and the streets of our community.

THE GHOST OF CHRISTMAS PRESENT

Two incidents stand out in my memory that taught me much about the challenges of this time in our lives and the lives of our children. Our daughter Havi was three years old and Michael was just a baby when we experienced our first test. While shopping one day in the Sherman Oaks Galleria, we came upon Santa Claus, sitting regally on his velvet throne, asking little children what they wanted for Christmas—while the moment was recorded for posterity by Santa's elves and their Polaroid cameras. My first reaction was to turn around and avoid passing the scene. But Havi had already noticed the action, and, of course, asked if she could "see" Santa Claus. No harm in that, we thought. So, we watched the joyful faces of the children as they sat on Santa's knee. "This is part of their holiday," we explained to Havi. "Oh, I know. They're Christmas," she replied."I'm Hanukkah."

We were lucky.

One year, we were driving through a part of town that seemed to have an unusual number of homes that were elaborately decorated for Christmas. "Oh, look at the beautiful lights!," Michael exclaimed."They're not so beautiful," I replied. Susie looked at me incredulously as if to say, "How can you say that? They are beautiful." But, as much as I hated to admit it, I felt threatened by the remark. Somehow, my darkest fears that the majority culture would steal my children's Jewish identity led me to deny the perfectly obvious fact that Christmas lights are indeed beautiful. Yet, my fears seemed justified when Michael asked, "Can we have lights on our house, too?"

"No," Susie said. "Those families are Christians, and they are celebrating their holiday of Christmas. We are Jewish, and Christmas is not our holiday. It's sort of like when you went to Josh's birthday party. Remember how you felt? You wanted it to be your party, but it wasn't. Your birthday is coming soon. But, you could still have fun at Josh's party, watching him open his presents and blowing out his candles. Well, these people are having a party called Christmas, but it's not our party. So, it wouldn't be right for us to put lights on our house. We will light the *ḥanukkiyah* on Ḥanukkah. That's our party."

The kids seemed to understand. Then, Havi asked, "Can we look at the lights on other houses?"

When we got home, I realized that I was the only person having problems with Christmas. Havi and Michael were taking everything in stride. If the argument Susie had developed made sense, then there was no reason not to acknowledge the beauty of Christmas decorations. There was a difference between allowing the kids to sit on Santa's knee, something we never did, and admiring the celebration of Christmas. It was the difference between appreciation and appropriation. So, the next evening, we piled the kids in the car and drove to a street in a neighboring community that the residents had turned into "Santa's Lane," complete with tremendous displays of Christmas decorations. We "oohed" and "ahhed" at the houses, then went for ice cream.

The kids never asked to do it again.

These personal reflections have helped shape this book. It is absolutely clear to me that Ḥanukkah in North America has become, and will continue to be, one of the most popular of Jewish holidays, if not the most popular, even though it is considered a minor holiday in the hierarchy of Jewish celebration. In fact, the most recent demographic surveys indicate that nearly 90% of North American Jews report lighting Ḥanukkah candles, while less than 40% say they light Shabbat candles. If the current trend continues, Ḥanukkah may overtake attending the Passover Seder as the most observed Jewish celebration.

There are significant reasons for this. Ḥanukkah is widely considered a "children's" holiday. Its celebration is quite joyful, centering on lights, presents, games and tasty foods. Compared to Passover or Shabbat, the amount of ritual required to observe the holiday is rather meager. The only required ritual action is to light candles each night and recite two (three on the first night) blessings. Even with the singing of traditional songs, the entire ceremony is completed in a manner of minutes. It is a very easy holiday to observe.

Yet, as in my own experience, parents of young children often go to great lengths to expand the simple Ḥanukkah celebration into an eight-night extravaganza. Undoubtedly, the influence of Christmas and the perceived need of Jewish parents to combat it with an elaborate Ḥanukkah celebration has contributed to the transformation of Ḥanukkah into a major Jewish holiday.

It would be fair to say that there is some controversy over whether the enhancement of Ḥanukkah is a good thing or a bad thing. Some argue that it is a distortion of the relative importance of the Jewish holidays to elevate Hanukkah to the same level as the three pilgrimage festivals—Passover, Shavuot, and Sukkot—or the High Holy Days, or even Shabbat. Others contend that throughout Jewish history, different holidays have held greater or lesser significance for Jews depending on the situation faced by the community.

In the Middle Ages, for example, when Jews lived in ghettos and under the constant fear of physical attack, Purim was a much more popular holiday than Hanukkah. Recall that Esther and Mordecai saved the Jews from Haman, a tyrant who planned to kill the Jews. Purim celebrates the rescue of Jews from the threat of physical annihilation. As we shall learn, Hanukkah celebrates the rescue of Judaism itself from the clutches of cultural assimilation. The ruling Syrian-Greeks sought to eliminate Judaism by encouraging Jews to give up their Jewish identities, primarily by attracting them with the enticements of the Hellenistic civilization. In our own day, living in a completely open society, we too must battle the forces of cultural assimilation to retain our Jewish identities. That is why so many Jews abhor the introduction of Christmas into the public arena and even into the Jewish family itself. That is why the lesson of Hanukkah—to fight for the right to be different, to fight for religious freedom—is so important today. That is why Hanukkah ought to be one of the most popular of Jewish holidays—but only if its true meaning and importance inform its celebration.

DISCOVERING THE ART OF CONTEMPORARY HANUKKAH CELEBRATION

Once again, we have approached the issue as the Rabbis of the Talmud are said to have done centuries ago when deciding difficult questions of Jewish practice - go listen to the people. The families we interviewed for this book reflect the diversity of opinion about the celebration of Hanukkah and the defense against Christmas. Some opt for minimizing the holiday, while others "go all out" in their Hanukkah celebrations. Some avoid the problem of Christmas by leaving town; others have spent years developing strategies for dealing with complex family situations in a way that is true to their Jewish commitments, yet sensitive to the needs of Christian members of the extended family.

I believe that our task is to infuse our celebration of Hanukkah with new meaning, new relevance, and new enthusiasm as part of our ongoing commitment to a vibrant Jewish life. I, for one, am not concerned that enhanced Hanukkah celebrations will overshadow other Jewish holidays, especially if we teach ourselves and our children the true meanings and lessons of the holiday. In view of the tremendous challenge of maintaining our Jewish commitments in an open society, a positive celebration of Hanukkah, along with observance of the other Jewish holidays and life cycle events, can only help our families to resist the forces of assimilation.

The stakes are high, for the celebration of Hanukkah, and the inevitable confrontation with Christmas, take place in our homes, in our families. It is in our families that we first acquire our Jewish identity. When Havi said to us "I'm Hanukkah," she was expressing a three-year-old's understanding that being Jewish is being different. Clearly, "being different" can be felt as a positive or a negative. The positive celebration of Hanukkah and the rest of the Jewish holidays can make being different very special indeed. We parents and grandparents are the first and most important teachers of Judaism and Jewish identity. The goal of this book is to equip our families with the tools to celebrate Hanukkah — meaningfully, creatively, joyously—as we continue to learn the art of Jewish living.

THE ART OF JEWISH LIVING

The Art of Jewish Living series began as the brainchild of Jules Porter when he was about to become the International President of the Federation of Jewish Men's Clubs. His dream was to create a library of practical guides to the celebration of Jewish life in the home and the synagogue, written for and taught by lay people in classes, seminars and workshops. The publication of *The Art of Jewish Living: The Shabbat Seder* (1985) and *The Art of Jewish Living: The Passover Seder* (1988) and now *The Art of Jewish Living: Hanukkah* (1990), along with supplementary workbooks, audio tapes, and teacher's guides, has indeed provided useful information for those seeking to move from the periphery into the center of Jewish life.

Thus, as always, the first *todah rabah* must go to Jules Porter. During the intervening years since the publication of *The AJL: The Passover Seder*, Jules has guided the Art of Jewish Living project with wisdom and skill. In addition to the successful completion of the Hanukkah volume, Jules responded to the historic exodus of Jews from the Soviet Union by authorizing the publication of a Russian language edition of *The Art of Jewish Living: The Passover Seder*. All this was in addition to his continuing work on behalf of the Conservative Movement, both in North America and in Israel. He is a remarkable leader, mentor, and *mensch*.

In the half-decade that I have been associated with the Federation of Jewish Men's Clubs, I've been continually amazed at the vitality and enthusiasm of its leadership and membership. Guided ably by its Executive Director, Rabbi Charles Simon—an exceptionally talented professional—the FJMC has shown tremendous vision in the projects with which it associates. I particularly want to thank the dedicated men who have served as President of the FJMC as the Art of Jewish Living project has grown: Mr. Joseph Gurmankin, Mr. Jules Porter, Dr. Jerome Agrest, and Mr. Lawrence Allen.

The Art of Jewish Living series has been embraced by every arm of the Conservative Movement: the Rabbinical Assembly, the Women's League for Conservative Judaism, the United Synagogue of America, the Jewish Theological Seminary of America, and, of course, the Federation of Jewish Men's Clubs.

Fifteen years ago, I was offered a faculty appointment at the University of Judaism, then a very small school of Jewish studies occupying a rather dilapidated old building in a rather dilapidated part of downtown Hollywood. Today, the University of Judaism is one of the major institutions of higher Jewish learning in the world, serving thousands of students yearly in its undergraduate, graduate, and adult education programs on its magnificent campus in the mountains of Bel Air. I am deeply grateful to the professional and lay leadership of the UJ for supporting my involvement with the Art of Jewish Living project—the President of the University, Dr. David Lieber, the Chairman of the Board of Directors, Mr. Jack M. Ostrow, and all of my colleagues, especially Dr. Elliot Dorff, Dr. Elieser Slomovic, Rabbi Daniel Gordis, and Rabbi Neal Weinberg. Special thanks to Rabbi Joel Roth, Rabbi Joel Rembaum, Professor Shaye Cohen, Dr. Egon Mayer, and Ms. Lydia Kukoff for reviewing portions of the manuscript, and to Beth Haber and Michael Wolf for lending their unique insights into the art and celebration of Hanukkah.

I am honored that my own rabbi, Harold M. Schulweis, one of the world's outstanding rabbinic leaders, graciously agreed to contribute the Preface to the volume.

The families and individuals who allowed me into their homes to share their Hanukkah experiences deserve special recognition: Claudia, Shlomo, David, Alissa, and Karen Bobrow; Rae and Jack Gindi; Ann, Jonathan, Adam, and Jennifer Kirsch; Elke, Rosa, Hester, and Orly Coblens; Lila and Sheldon Schein; Carol and Eric Mills; and members of my *havurah*, Debbie and Larry Neinstein, Bonnie and Ira Goodberg, Janice and Ben Reznik, Tobi and Nahum Inlander, Beverly Weise, and Judy and Herschel Fox.

Once again, the creative wizards who make the Art of Jewish Living series such a warm and inviting visual experience are to be thanked. Jules Porter provided all the beautiful photography, Carolyn Moore Mooso edited the copy, and the talented designers at Alef Type and Design, Jane Golub, Alan Rowe, and Ira Wise, gave the book its shape and look.

Joel Lurie Grishaver is widely known as this generation's most creative curriculum developer in Jewish education. Yet, his genius is recognized mainly by those who employ his dozens of publications in Jewish religious schools throughout the world. Truth be told, to the thousands of Jewish children who study Torah and learn about Judaism through the pages of his books, Joel is a hero who makes Jewish learning a joy. The chapter on "The Ever-Evolving Story of Hanukkah" is based on Joel's earlier work in this area. I am especially pleased that much of the adult Jewish world has been exposed to Joel's brilliance through his editing of the Art of Jewish Living series.

One of the great dangers for someone who works professionally as a Jewish family educator is that one's own family must often endure extra hours at the computer and many *Shabbatot* without Dad when he is off teaching. I am truly blessed with two terrific children, Havi and Michael, and a wonderful wife, Susie, who offer me only understanding and support as I continue my work. Thanks for your love.

Ron Wolfson
Los Angeles, California
Elul 5750
September, 1990

USING THIS TEXT

There are two major parts to this text. *Part I: The Art of Hanukkah* presents the steps required for the traditional celebration of Hanukkah, complete with information about the candlelighting ceremony, foods, gifts, songs, and games associated with the holiday. *Part II: The December Dilemmas* tackles the often difficult issues that surface because of the proximity of Hanukkah to Christmas.

In each section of the book, we hear from real Jewish families interviewed for this project as they talk about their experiences with the celebration of Hanukkah. We hope their insights and examples will resonate with the reader's.

Hanukkah is a relatively simple holiday to celebrate. The central ritual is lighting the Hanukkah candles each of eight consecutive nights. In **Part I**, we explore the "Concepts" and "Objects" of the celebration and then teach the "Practice" of the ritual itself. Once again, we divide the Hebrew texts of the blessings and songs of Hanukkah into small word phrases and number them in a linear fashion. We then present them in a three-column format. From right to left across the pages, they are: 1) the Hebrew text, 2) the English translation of the text, and 3) the English transliteration of the text. This allows those who are able to read the original language to work with it and the English translation column, while those who cannot read the original Hebrew can work with the English transliteration and translation columns. This linear presentation should assist the learner in deciphering the meaning of the Hebrew words.

The transliteration scheme generally follows that used by the Rabbinical Assembly in its recent prayer books:

ai	=	as in "I" —*Adonai*	=	ah-doe-n'I
ei	=	as in "hay" —*Eloheinu*	=	eh-low-hay-nu
i	=	as in "see" —*l'hadlik*	=	leh-hahd-leek
o	=	as in "low" —*shalom*	=	shah-lowm
e	=	as in "red" —*Elohim*	=	eh-low-heem
a	=	as in "Mama" —*bara*	=	bah-rah
u	=	as in "blue" —*vanu*	=	vah-nu
kh	=	as in the sound you make when trying to dislodge a fishbone from the roof of your mouth		
h	=	also as in the sound you make when trying to dislodge a fishbone from the roof of your mouth		

Following the texts, a section entitled "Practical Questions and Answers" poses and answers common questions about the celebration of Hanukkah.

Part II: The December Dilemmas begins with comments from our model families about their struggles with the winter holiday season and then offers an extended essay on the issues that make up the December Dilemmas.

A selected bibliography only hints at the multitude of resources available for those interested in learning more about Hanukkah.

B'hatzlahah! We wish you "success" learning the Art of Jewish Living.

PART I
THE ART OF HANUKKAH

1
WHAT IS HANUKKAH?

I don't know what I think—but in the real world Hanukkah is a very important holiday and everybody goes crazy over Hanukkah because they get a lot of presents and they get to stuff their mouths with delicious food made with oil which makes them fat. I don't know what it is for me.

Karen Bobrow

"WHAT IS HANUKKAH?"

This simple question, "What is Hanukkah?," begins the Talmud's brief discussion of Hanukkah. For those rabbinic sages in Babylonia who were busy creating the future of Judaism, the Judaism we now practice, the question was not rhetorical. It wasn't for pedagogic purposes. Gathered in Babylonia, some three or four hundred years after the original event, the rabbis had some serious questions about the true meaning of a holiday which was widely celebrated, but whose central message was less than clear. For the rabbis the meaning and purpose of Hanukkah was indeed in doubt; so was its authenticity. Hanukkah wasn't in the Torah, it wasn't part of the Bible, it wasn't a clear and obvious *mitzvah* (commandment) from God. Instead, Hanukkah celebrated the political and social independence of a country which had long since been destroyed. In many ways, it was false pride and an inappropriate reliance on the memories of military victories past which led to its fall. It made heroes of the Hasmonean dynasty, a dynasty which after the "Judah" generation turned into some of the cruelest and most hateful of all the Israelite kings. Yet, Hanukkah was something which every Jew celebrated—it was a very popular holiday. The rabbis' challenge was to give this common practice a viable meaning, one which was worth holding onto and celebrating.

Their solution was to center the celebration of Hanukkah on "the miracle of the oil," an event which involved God's intervention and kept the celebration's central focus far away from the Maccabees and their victories. It made Hanukkah a holiday which celebrates how God helps us "when our own strength fails us."

When we approached writing this book on modern Hanukkah practice, we began with the same question, "What is Hanukkah?" For us, too, the question was not a self-obvious introduction. It was not a pedagogic prompt. In our day and age, Hanukkah has become the premier public Jewish holiday, the one most obviously celebrated, and the one whose practical meaning has become most obscure. More than 1500 years in Christian society had shifted Hanukkah's meaning and purpose. Hanukkah had grown and mutated, faced off against Christmas, retreated, and then reentered the struggle.

It is very clear to us that the "true meaning" of Hanukkah is again on the move, and with it, the ways Hanukkah is celebrated. In researching this book, as we have done with each of the other Art of Jewish Living volumes, we followed the rabbinic dictum: *Tzei U-l'mad,* "go and learn." As the rabbis did when they faced problems of practice, we went and looked at what the average Jew (and in our case, some very special Jews) was already doing. When we looked at their practice and their understandings, we found some very interesting common threads.

a. The very lack of definition of specific Hanukkah practice frees families and empowers tremendous creativity. In many senses, Hanukkah is a much more comfortable holiday, because it doesn't come with the same kinds of formal guidelines and expectations as does Passover.

b. Even for families who are very secure in their Jewishness, Christmas represents a perceived threat. In each of the interviews we held, the topic of resisting Christmas took up far more time than did the observance of Hanukkah.

c. It has become a North American tradition to maximize the Hanukkah experience (out of competition with Christmas). North American Jews have evolved a kind of Super-Hanukkah celebration with "eight nights' worth of presents," major decorations, a huge family gathering, etc. These actions are designed to foster "Jewish pride," especially for the children. However, for some of the families we interviewed, this Super-Hanukkah experience has begun to feel overblown and artificial. It seems to them that it has come to manifest "insecurity" rather than "pride," so they have begun a process of "cooling" their Hanukkah celebrations.

d. In the late 1960's, thanks to the Supreme Court of the United States, we thought we had finally won the battle to keep Christmas out of our children's public schools. The separation between Church and State seemed clear. Today, some of our fellow Jews, with their successful legal fights to permit the display of *hanukkiyot* in public space, have helped to erode that separation. Even more caustic to our integrity is the benign insensitivity of many of those in the public sector. Amazingly, the non-day-school children we interviewed are still faced with the ethnic/ethical dilemma of which words to mouth during winter recitals and concerts.

e. The Christmas tree once served as an effective boundary line. It served as a way of separating the "real" Jews from those who would rapidly disappear. Although some Jews did have decorated bushes and trees, they were kept with a certain embarrassment which acknowledged the boundary as they crossed it. Today, almost every Jewish family has non-Jewish relatives who respectfully and appropriately celebrate Christmas. The boundary between "us" and "them" has been blurred—Hanukkah and Christmas are now related by marriage, and keeping them distinct, if not apart, represents a new and formidable challenge.

Ann, Jonathan, Adam and Jennifer Kirsch

The Kirsch family delightfully mixes the intellectual world of books, the emotional fervor of psychotherapy, the developmental craziness of adolescence, the innocence of middle childhood, and a deeply felt devotion to things Jewish. Their stories of Hanukkah reflect the mainstream concerns of Jewish families: purpose, presents, parties, public schools—and Christmas.

Jonathan is an attorney in private practice and, following in the footsteps of his remarkable father, the late Robert Kirsch, writes weekly book reviews for the Los Angeles Times. Ann works as a psychotherapist, specializing in early childhood development. Adam, 14, is a sophomore at a public high school and Jennifer, a precocious 8, attends a public elementary school. Active in a local Conservative synagogue, Adat Shalom, the Kirsches have struggled with the issues of the winter holidays in the public schools and the practice of giving presents, while creating a marvelous holiday celebration for their family and friends.

YOUR AUTHOR: So tell me, we just celebrated Hanukkah. What is the nicest thing about Hanukkah for you?

JENNIFER: I would have to say the last night when we have our party. Usually we invite about thirty people and everybody brings a menorah and we light them over on that table and we sing songs and usually there are a lot of kids, little kids. So, me and my friends usually take care of them while the grownups talk and we have a dessert buffet....

JONATHAN: We faced this big crisis about three years ago because it was clear that there were just too many presents. The kids would get overly anxious about it; they would just be in a frenzy. Even we got caught up in it. We would worry and fret about having eight really good gifts—a gift every night. There was just this terrible tension about whether you should open one or open two and if you open two are you going to have one for each night?... So, we had a big confrontation about it and we decided that the point of Hanukkah was not the giving of gifts; that was the point of Christmas. We decided that we would put one or two of the gifts out on the first night. They could open them at once, or, if they chose they could wait. Each night thereafter we would give what I understand to be the traditional Hanukkah gift which is gelt. This has made a tremendous difference in my perception in the way the holiday is celebrated in this house. It is a much more pleasant and meaningful celebration for us.

ANN: I think that the problem was mainly mine or mainly ours. It was our wanting to give to our kids. Our wanting to have this wonderful show. I remember when I was growing up and seeing all of these presents piled up and how much I loved that. Well, one year I did not love it anymore. It happened very abruptly. It wasn't anything in particular that was done or wasn't done. It was just this sense that both Jonathan and I came to that this was not going to do. When we sat down and explained all of this to the kids, they did not have a problem. It was really amazing. I expected a lot of anguish and hysteria about it, but they understood completely what we were saying. The true test, of course, was the next year at Hanukkah. We discussed how we were going to do it and there wasn't an argument. It was as if we took that whole burden off of everybody and it was okay with everybody to not spend eight hysterical anxious days.

ADAM: I am fourteen now and there is not really very much that I want. I think that made a difference too. The most that I could ask for was maybe a book or two and the rest money.

JENNIFER: I think that my biggest problem was that I wanted to open a lot of presents on the first night. But Adam wanted to wait and open one each night. I didn't think it was fair that he got to open a present when I didn't have one. Now that we open all the presents on the first night, it's okay.

JONATHAN: What we concentrate on now is that Hanukkah is a time to be with our friends and our family. We have friends that every year invite us to their house for one night and they come to our house. My folks have us over. Some nights it's just us. The big event of Hanukkah for us is the eighth night which has become a tradition. We invite our family and friends for a big celebration. Everyone brings a *hanukkiyah*; this year we must have had twenty. Since it is the eighth night, each *hanukkiyah* is filled with eight lights. It is a great spectacle, one of the few Jewish holiday spectacles of the year in our home and the kids are always very entranced by it. With the sight of so many lights burning, I am personally entranced.

YOUR AUTHOR: How many years have you done this?

JONATHAN: Probably ten years. People so look forward to it, they call just to make sure what night we're doing the party. We always try to invite new people, people that we might hear of who don't have family in town or don't have a Hanukkah celebration.

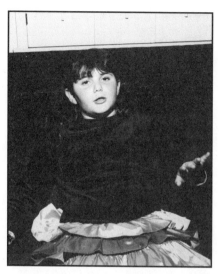

ANN: We have one friend who grew up in a family that did not celebrate much of anything. She thinks they had a menorah but she isn't really sure. It was the kind of thing that if they remembered to take it down, they would light it. Now that she has been coming to our home, this year she went out and bought a menorah. I asked her why. She explained that in the past she was afraid of it because she was afraid that she could not do it right. She was not coming from an observant family so she did not know what was right and what was wrong. Many Jews are afraid to ask how to do things because they are afraid to show that they do not know. When she purchased a menorah, it was quite a moment for her. She also started inviting some people over for Shabbat dinners and she started going to different *shuls* around town to see what they are all about. She is making some tentative steps towards the direction of finding out what Judaism means for her.

Rae and Jack Gindi

Rae and Jack Gindi can be officially called "empty-nesters," but their nest fre-quently features the sounds of their four adult children and six grandchildren who live nearby. Well-known philanthropists and leaders of the Los Angeles Jewish com-munity, the Gindis have fashioned a home filled with original Jewish art, commis-sioned Jewish books, and beautiful Jewish ritual objects that reflect their devotion to Judaism and the Jewish people.

Tracing their ancestry from Turkey, to Syria, to Brooklyn, to New Orleans, to Los Angeles, Jack and Rae are steeped in the colorful traditions of their Sephardic her-itage. Special songs, unusual foods, and customized <u>h</u>anukkiyot all reflect their ancestral roots in the celebration of <u>H</u>anukkah. Yet, after years of living in a com-munity dominated by Jews with East European origins, their <u>H</u>anukkah celebrations combine the best of both Sephardi and Ashkenazi traditions.

YOUR AUTHOR: Why does your *hanukkiyah* have two *shamashim?*

RAE: When my ancestors came from Turkey and settled in Aleppo, Syria, they were not trusted by the other Jews as being completely kosher. Once they were accepted into the community, they were so grateful that when Hanukkah came, they lit a second *shamash.* It became a tradition. Another reason is because we are in the Diaspora, we will light two *shamashim* until such time as we go back to Israel. We have had most of our *hanukkiyot* custom-made with two places for the *shamashim.*

JACK: I remember the pastries on Hanukkah. In those days, nobody had dinners to celebrate holidays because they could not afford it. So, you had a sweet table for guests. It is like when you go to visit in Israel, the people set out a sweet table. On holidays like Rosh Ha-Shanah or before Yom Kippur you had meals, but for the others, when the family got together, it was a very elaborate sweet table.

YOUR AUTHOR: Since both of you grew up in the Sephardic tradition, how did the Ashkenazi traditions come in?

RAE: Through our involvement at the University of Judaism. And our kids have attended religious school with mostly Ashkenazi children. I learned how to make latkes when the kids were in nursery school. We have incorporated some Ashkenazic customs, but we keep a lot of our Syrian traditions.

YOUR AUTHOR: So, what will you serve at your Hanukkah party?

RAE: Well, we'll have Ashkenazi latkes, some chicken, and a fabulous Sephardic dish called *kibbeh.*

YOUR AUTHOR: What is *kibbeh?*

RAE: You get it in Moroccan restaurants. It looks like a torpedo, stuffed with meat.

JACK: Our celebration of Hanukkah is much more festive than when I was a kid. Then, you had big family gatherings at Passover and the High Holidays. Not at Hanukkah. Hanukkah was spent alone, just with your immediate family. It was not a major holiday. That is the biggest change. Now, we have big Hanukkah parties with families and friends.

RAE: This year, our Ḥanukkah party will be Sunday night, the third night of Ḥanukkah. Yes, it's also Christmas Eve, but two nights are Shabbat, and the kids have a party at school on another night. I know a lot of families get together on Christmas Day, but we want to light the candles at night, according to the tradition. With all the *ḥanukkiyot*, it's quite beautiful.

Claudia, Shlomo, David, Alissa, and Karen Bobrow

Claudia Carlson grew up in a Lutheran family in Northern California. Shlomo Bobrow was born in Russia and raised in a secular Israeli family in Holon. They met when friends took them to a Hanukkah latke party at the Chabad House in Los Angeles.

Eighteen years later, they are a happily married couple, having created a fully observant Jewish home for themselves and their three children. Extremely active

in the life of their synagogue, Valley Beth Shalom, Claudia and Shlomo are members of a havurah, take leadership roles in the congregation, and participate in the alternative Library Minyan. David recently celebrated his Bar Mitzvah and attends a Jewish day high school. Alissa, 11, and Karen, 9, are students at the synagogue day school.

Reflecting an oft-repeated story, Claudia's conversion to Judaism also prompted Shlomo's commitment to Jewish religious life. A sensitive teacher and writer, Claudia has a deep love for Jewish ideas and observances that has guided the family's ever-increasing Jewish practice. Yet, the winter holidays bring the family face-to-face with the fact that while Claudia converted to Judaism, her family did not. Negotiating the icy roads of December can be tricky, even in Southern California. The Bobrows' solution to their family's December Dilemmas has been reached after years of debate and experimentation.

SHLOMO: My first real memories of celebrating <u>H</u>anukkah are from Israel. When we came to Israel, we sang songs and lit candles and ate *pontshkes*. *Pontshke* is a jelly doughnut, what we call now *sufganiyot*. It is really puffy and light, not like the jelly doughnuts that we have here.

CLAUDIA: I knew when I converted that Christmas was no longer going to be part of my life. That was obvious to me because we had discussed it. I had another Jewish boyfriend before Shlomo and we had discussed the problem so I knew where Jews were coming from on this issue. You cannot have a Christmas tree if you are Jewish. That was pretty clear to me. When I met Shlomo, he also was very adamantly opposed to a Christmas tree—so I knew up front that Christmas was going to go.

I am trying to remember what happened the first year that I was Jewish. I don't even remember. You block these things from your mind. The first years were very difficult because I had all of these Christmas traditions. My family made lovely little cookies and fruit cake. There was rice pudding and we decorated the tree and we had stockings. Now, I didn't have a stocking or a decorated tree, but I realized I didn't have to cut everything out. Just because you didn't have a tree didn't mean you could not have cookies. I went ahead and I

made cookies. I don't think I made rice pudding. Shlomo came home with a bunch of jelly donuts which I was not very impressed with. I woke up with indigestion. I made latkes that I don't think came out very good that year. I really did not know what I was doing but I fumbled my way through it.

I lit candles, but you know, when you don't have any background in what you are doing, it takes a while to do. Plus, Shlomo did not come from an American family where he had a strong tradition of all kinds of Hanukkah customs from home. We were both sort of standing there thinking "Well, what do we do now?"

At first, we solved the problem of Christmas by leaving town. One year we went to the Grand Canyon. One year we went to New York to be with Shlomo's Jewish relatives. It was an ideal time for us to go and visit them. So Christmas sort of got pushed off to the side and it was not an issue for those couple of years. But after I had David, I realized we were not going to be traveling with a little baby and that we were going to have to somehow work this out with my family. It was self-evident that Hanukkah and Christmas were falling at the same time every year. You could not pretend that Christmas didn't exist because my family was still celebrating every year.

We did not talk about it in my family, which I think might have been a mistake. But I did not feel comfortable talking about it and I don't think they felt comfortable talking about it and they did not know what to say. They were kind of at a loss. My family was very positive about my conversion to Judaism. It wasn't as if I had someone standing behind me all the time asking "Why did you do this?" or "This is a terrible thing" or "We will never speak to you again." It was nothing like that. They were very positive and very good about it. They were just not sure how to handle things.

The smart thing would have been to sit down as a group and discuss this and come up with some conclusions on how to do this. The way it would work out was that we would go to them for Christmas. But they would have their cold table every year on Christmas Day which had all the Danish kinds of cheeses and shrimp salad and pork salami and we had a problem right from the start because we were not eating any of those things.

YOUR AUTHOR: What's a "cold table?"

CLAUDIA: It is the Danish version of a smorgasbord. They have schnapps and beer. We would just avoid some of the foods and we managed and kind of muddled our way through it. They would give me gifts wrapped in blue and white paper.

Still, every year we had this discussion about what to do about Christmas. Finally about five years ago, my mother said "I think we need to know where we are coming from on this gift thing. How are we going to do this? Are we going to have all of the gifts at Christmas or are we going to have all of the gifts on Hanukkah." She said, "You figure out however you want to do it and we will go along with you." So we all thought about it and we finally decided that what we would do was they would come to us for Hanukkah every year. I would make latkes. I would make cookies. We would light candles and we would eat whatever and we would sit around and sing Hanukkah songs and they would bring gifts to us. Then at Christmas we would go to their house. We would eat rice pudding and the cookies that she makes. They would light the Christmas tree. We would listen to Christmas carols and we would give them their gifts.

Elke, Rosa, Hester, and Orly Coblens

Elke Coblens is a single mom. After her husband Steve died, Elke faced the task of reconstructing her life with three young daughters. With remarkable courage and dedication, she has infused her family with warmth, caring, and a continuing commitment to Jewish involvement.

The Coblens' Hanukkah celebration is a creative combination of lights, latkes, and loving, albeit unusual, gifts. Where else in the world could you find a family dedicating one night of Hanukkah to earthquake gifts!? Rosa, 13, Hester, 11, and Orly, 6, all attend Jewish day schools and Camp Ramah. Elke is a former educator, now businesswoman, active in her synagogue, Adat Ari El, and communal Jewish life. Surrounded by a loving community of family and friends, Elke and her girls find ways to increase the light of Hanukkah.

ROSA: The first night is "sister" night.

YOUR
AUTHOR: What does that mean?

ROSA: My Mom used to buy a present from Hester to me and Orly to me and buy presents from me to Hester and Orly, but this year on sister night, Hester and Orly bought me a present and I bought Hester and Orly each a present.

YOUR AUTHOR: So first night is sister night. Is there a special second night?

HESTER: Not in order. We never know what to expect.

ORLY: There is "book" night and "shoe" night.

YOUR AUTHOR: What does that mean?

ORLY: On book night we get books for Hanukkah. We each get four books.

HESTER: On shoe night, we get a pair of shoes.

YOUR AUTHOR: Any other nights?

ORLY: Last year, we had "earthquake" night. My mommy gave me an earthquake gift. We each have one to put by our beds....safety flares, batteries, and a radio and a flashlight, gloves and a mask. That was great!

YOUR AUTHOR: Okay, any other nights besides sister, book, shoes, and earthquake?

ROSA: Well, there is one night for my Mom's side of the family and one night for my Dad's side of the family and then there is a night we give to our Mom—that is family night.

YOUR AUTHOR: So, do you stack the presents somewhere in the house or do they come out?

HESTER: They come out of my Mom's room.

ELKE: There is a time prior to Hanukkah that you cannot enter my room anymore...

I grew up in a family where my mother believed in giving presents every night; why, I don't know. Even if it was just a pair of socks. It never had to be something major—just the fact of doing it.

Hanukkah is a big deal, but it is not the same big deal as Rosh Ha-Shanah or Pesah. With Pesah, the big deal is with all the preparation and all the hubbub that goes into it.

It's been great watching Rosa's feelings about Hanukkah change. Now that she is babysitting and earning some of her own money, she really loves buying her sisters and others Hanukkah presents. She loves that a lot. She does it just for the sake of giving. I don't see her wanting to do that for birthdays. I buy them birthday presents from each other, but she makes a point of doing that for Hanukkah...

YOUR AUTHOR: How is Hanukkah for you as a single parent?

ELKE: I think it is tough. Life is really hard as a single parent. Some singles I talk to think it has been a real struggle for them to keep the Jewish stuff alive in the kind of way that they want to because they feel that so much of the celebrations are centered around family. By "family" they mean two parents, three kids—that kind of thing. It is painful for them, they would rather not do it, or they would rather let someone else in the family do it for them.

It is real interesting because in my family, I am the one who does it all. I do both nights of Rosh Ha-Shanah, I do both *sedarim*. I am it, for whatever reason. My father passed away three months before Steve. We used to go to my mother one night and either we would have it one night or we would go to my in-laws when they were still living in the L.A. area. I sort of took over.

I guess I had the need Jewishly to have as few changes in my children's life as possible—and just because Steve wasn't here, just because there wasn't a male here—did not mean that we could not do all of the things that we did all along.

2
The Ever-Evolving Story of Hanukkah

It is about the Jews and they were not allowed to practice their own religion so they ganged up against the king of Syria and it was hard and there were a few of them. They were the Maccabees and they won and they came to the Temple and they rededicated it because it was all messed up and the Bibles and everything in it. That is basically why we have Hanukkah.

Alissa Bobrow

It was the time of the Second Temple and the Syrians were in with the Greeks, whatever, and the Greeks put them in charge of all of the area around Israel. They made it so they could not practice their religion. So then some of the Maccabees rebelled and they won. They went to the Temple.

Karen Bobrow

It was Alexander that let them practice their religion. He made them get freedom and it was the other Greeks who came, like Antiochus. He did not let them practice. We celebrate for eight nights because the Maccabees, since they were rebels fighting, they did not have a chance to celebrate Sukkot, so they made Hanukkah kind of like Sukkot. Sukkot was for eight days and since they could not celebrate Sukkot they made another holiday for eight days.

David Bobrow

American Jewry has recreated Hanukkah in its own image. This reshaping is not just a question of Styrofoam, glitter, strings of flashing lights, and eight nights' worth of presents. Rather, it goes right to the heart of our very understanding of Hanukkah's meanings and lessons.

MATTATHIAS WASHINGTON AND THE COLONIAL MACCABEES

For Jews, Hanukkah is essentially an oral holiday. Every Jewish community, every family, is left to retell the story on their own. There is no Hanukkah Haggadah, we have no Hanukkah Seder; rather, we are left with nine candles, the one-line *b'rakhot*, a couple of very short prayers and a song or two. With these limited tools, each family is asked to breathe into Hanukkah the breath of life.

Even when we check the authorized Jewish sources, there is only one official Hanukkah text (of any authority). There is no mention of Hanukkah in our Bible (though ironically the Catholic Bible does include the Books of the Maccabees.) There is no book of Hanukkah in the Mishnah. Only when we reach the Gemara (the second layer of the Talmud) do we find a single passage which explains Hanukkah's history and meaning (though a couple of other passages do define Hanukkah's practices). This single passage is hidden in the midst of a discussion of candle wicks in the book devoted to Shabbat.

For the rabbis, the original founders of modern Judaism, Hanukkah wasn't important enough to merit a book of its own. Or perhaps, as we will see, they wanted to make sure that in the future, Hanukkah wouldn't be important enough to merit a book of its own. In any case, the official Jewish version of the Hanukkah story is this:

What is Hanukkah?

Our rabbis taught: On the twenty-fifth of Kislev begins the eight days of Hanukkah, which are days on which mourning and fasting are prohibited.

For when the Greeks entered the Temple, they defiled all of the oil; and when the Hasmonean dynasty defeated them, they searched and found only one jug of oil with the official seal of the Head *Kohein* (Priest), enough to burn for one day. But a miracle happened and the oil lasted for eight days.

In the following years, these days were appointed as a festival on which Hallel was said.

Shabbat 21b

We American Jews like the Maccabees. (Israelis like them, too.) Where the rabbinic telling of this story centers on the "High Priest" and a miracle (and never even calls the family of Ḥashmon "the Maccabees"), we Americans like good old Judah "The Hammer" Maccabee. Our Ḥanukkah retellings are filled with a sense of his bravery and the cleverness of his guerilla strategies (even if we don't know any of the details). We see him (and his band of merry men) fighting hard in the mountains (often in the snow—though we rarely say that out-loud). In our hearts, we identify deeply with them. We can see ourselves fighting alongside them, just the way we can see ourselves alongside Johnny Tremaine and the rest of the Continental army, picking off the British Dragoons as they march past Robert Frost's stone walls on the way from Lexington to Concord. In our imagination, the Greeks are just as easy to ambush.

If you want to get to the heart of the All-American Ḥanukkah myth, take a look at the following American Jewish folk story:

It is mid-winter at Valley Forge. Everyone is cold. Frostbite is widespread. Everyone has given up hope. George Washington is depressed. One night, looking for inspiration, George goes for a walk through the camp. He finds one Jewish member of the Continental Army lighting his *ḥanukkiyah*. (Don't laugh. It works. Valley Forge was a winter event—Christmas time—so it was probably Ḥanukkah, too. And, based on our common knowledge of Hayyim Solomon's contribution to the American Revolution, there had to be at least one Jewish Revolutionary soldier.) The soldier explains Ḥanukkah, Judah Maccabee, and everything to George, who refinds his courage in the process— enough to stand up when the boat crosses the Delaware. Later, the first President sends our Jewish soldier a silver menorah (probably made by his friend Paul in Boston) as a gift of appreciation, along with a letter which says, "Judaism has a lot to offer the world. You should be proud to be a Jew."

I apologize for not knowing the true origin of this tale. I have encountered it many times in my life. I was told it as a story sermon in my boyhood. I have read it in various collections during my college days. (You can find one version of it in *Time for My Soul, A Treasury of Jewish Stories for Our Holy Days*, Annette and Eugene Labovitz, Jason Aronson, 1988). To the best of my knowledge it is a legitimate American Jewish folk tale. I'll even bet that it was created in the early fifties—it has all the markings of a post-World War II baby boom myth. It epitomizes the Americanization of Ḥanukkah, using George Washington as the "proof text" for two important lessons: (1) that Ḥanukkah is essentially the celebration of a successful revolution for freedom, just like the American Revolution, and (2) that Hanukkah should teach us to be proud of our Jewish tradition (and thus we should not be embarrassed by the attention paid to other celebrations during the winter season).

Even though these are good and true messages, neither of them has much to do with Hanukkah's original meaning. But, to tell the truth, neither did the little jug of oil 'that thought it could,' and then did last for eight nights. Like every important Jewish event, Hanukkah has many revisionist histories and many interpretations. This is a tribute to its richness and to the dynamic and fluid nature of the Jewish tradition. To understand all of this, let's go back before the beginning.

ACT ONE: GELT-RIDDEN

PRE-MACCABEAN ORIGINS

To understand Hanukkah, we need to start in Turkey. Before we can understand the religious issues, we need to understand the politics. Before we can understand the politics, we need to know a little about the economics.

Therefore, the Ever-Evolving Story of Hanukkah begins at the foot of Mt. T'molus. (Yes, it is a real place). Mt. T'molus was rich in gold, and gold dust washed off its slopes into the waters of the Pactolus River. Circa 1200 B.C.E., people would throw sheepskins into the river, allowing the gold dust to collect on the skin's oily hairs. Later the skins were burned in the fire and the gold dust would melt and be collected as nuggets. This practice probably gave birth to the legend of Jason and the Golden Fleece.

Later, people learned to pan the river for gold. The Greek historian Theophratus tells this story: One day a man panning for gold in the Pactolus River found a black rock. This rock had one unique property: When it was rubbed with gold, the gold left a streak. If the gold wasn't pure, you could tell by the color of the streak. This meant that people could now check out the purity of gold without melting things down.

Up to this moment, barter had been the dominant economic system. But, that was before the discovery of this rock. This rock was called the touchstone and it changed the world. Because of the touchstone, people began to use gold to trade with instead of apples, wheat, olives and other natural resources. Gold was better. It was more portable. And, best of all, gold wouldn't rot or spoil. With the use of gold, international trade really began to flourish. Eventually, gold was packaged in fixed sizes and called "money." Herodotus, circa 450 B.C.E. suggests that Gyges, King of Lydia, was the first to use touchstone technology to mint coins.

The next needed step was the international standardization of money. The man to do it was Alexander the Great. Alex was a short man (under 5'2") from a suburb of Greece called Macedonia. Alexander the Great set out from Macedonia and proceeded to conquer the entire known world. (This was no mean feat for a kind man of under 5'2".) Everywhere he went, Alexander brought the gifts of Greek culture. Philosophy, science, politics, theater were now making it on the international scene. Alexander forced no one to accept these gifts. Rather, he let everyone live in peace as long as they paid their taxes. But he did make the gifts of Greek culture available.

For Jews reading this text, it would be best at this moment if you would picture the Maccabean chorus whispering in unison: "Beware of Greeks bearing gifts."

MEANWHILE, BACK ON THE FARM

Meanwhile, Judea was a sleepy little rural state, filled with pastoral hamlets. Here, near to their places of birth, Jewish families lived under their vines and fig trees, dwelling in peace and unafraid, except for a few conquests...

In 928 B.C.E., after Solomon's death, the Land of Israel was split into two Kingdoms: Israel (ten of the tribes) and Judah (just the tribe of Judah and little Benjamin) when Jeroboam led a breakaway rebellion against Solomon's son, Rehoboam.

In 722 B.C.E., Tiglath-pileser III, the King of Assyria, conquered and destroyed Israel, leaving only Judah. The "Israelites" were carried away and vanished forever from Jewish history, leaving only Judah (and little Benjamin).

In the early 600's (B.C.E.), Assyria lost power. Its empire and the renewed Egyptian empire were slowly gobbled up by the new force on the scene, Babylonia. On the 9th of Av, 586 B.C.E., Nebuchadnezzar conquered Jerusalem, destroyed the Temple, and Judah fell. However, Jeremiah, the leading prophet of the era, prophesied that Babylonia, too, would fall—and that the Jews would be returned to their land in seventy years.

Jeremiah knew his stuff. In 539 B.C.E., Cyrus, the founding King of the Persian Empire, outmaneuvered Nabonidus (Nebuchadnezzar's heir) and took control of the Babylonian Empire, making it his own. One of his first actions was to give the Jews permission to return to Israel. In 458 B.C.E., a Jewish leader known as Ezra the Scribe took over leadership of this return to the Land of Israel and began the process of rebuilding the nation. One of the first items of business was the rebuilding of the Holy Temple.

As part of this national rebuilding effort, Ezra also began a parallel process of reconstructing Judaism. In the Talmud (*Bava Kamma* 82a) we find a list of his innovations:

Ten Fixes That Ezra Fixed (Or, Ten Practices That Ezra Practiced):

(1) That the Torah be read publicly at Shabbat *Minhah* Services.
(2) That the Torah be read publicly on Mondays and Thursdays.
(3) That courts be held on Mondays and Thursdays.
(4) That clothes be washed on Thursdays (in anticipation of Shabbat).
(5) That garlic (an aphrodisiac) be eaten on Friday

(6) That (on Friday) a housewife rise early to bake bread.
(7) That a woman must wear a *sinar* (probably a girdle, but no one actually knows).
(8) That a woman must comb her hair before going to the *mikvah* (ritual bath).
(9) That spice sellers be allowed to travel between towns.
(10) That a person who has a "pollution" must go to the *mikvah*.

Ezra's reforms dramatically changed Jewish life (or at least the Bible chronicles a dramatic change). The first two of these "fixes" established the public reading of Torah. Previously, the Torah had belonged to the Priests and public readings were limited to the small sections they chose to use liturgically. What had once been the "secret knowledge" of the cult was now thrown open to the people as a whole. In many, many ways, Rabbinic Judaism was started from this single act.

It would be nice to say that the Temple had been the central force in Jewish life before the Exile, and that the synagogue was invented in Babylon as a way of coping with its destruction—but that isn't precisely true. Even though *The New Jewish History* which I studied in fifth grade at Hebrew school taught it as a definitive truth, it is now clear that synagogue-like communal gatherings for local (non-Temple centered) worship experiences were evolving before the Babylonian exile. However, synagogues as an "institution" probably did grow in importance in Babylonia, and thereby influenced Ezra's reforms.

Intellectually, Judaism was now ready to grow and change. Ezra's reforms set the stage. Economically, most Judean Jews were still isolated farmers, living in small agricultural villages, but that was soon to change.

Alexander entered the Holy Land with that newfangled invention, money. Money, especially with his universally accepted picture on it, changed everything. Soon, people everywhere were giving up barter and beginning to specialize. All of a sudden, crafts were big business. Now, a person could spend all day spinning wool or throwing pots and still have bread on the table. All of a sudden, everyone didn't need to be a farmer. All at once, whole new kinds of cities were both possible and necessary. Because of money, Joe Judean, Nick Naphtali, Sam Simeon, Eddie Ephraim, Mark Manasseh, and lots of other Jewish kids left their farms and moved to the Big City-State. All of a sudden, every Jewish kid wanted to have a job.

In the city-state, the farm kids discovered a whole new way of life. There were lots of people living close together. It was a whole new kind of community. For the first time, people had affordable access to light after dark—because it was now possible to earn a reasonable living crushing olives and selling the oil. Money, craft-oriented jobs, and light after dark contributed to a whole new concept: LEISURE TIME.

The Greeks were the masters of leisure time. Think of all the good Greek stuff: the baths (later made famous by the Romans), the theater, the library, athletics and flaming-cheese—all of them are leisure time activities. Education, too, was an essential ethos of this Greek system, and with leisure time, systematic learning could also now became part of the daily schedule. As this happened, the former farm kids who were used to working from dawn to dusk (and who couldn't previously afford light after dark) were taken by the new possibilities. Suddenly, Joe Judean and his friends were faced with a choice: How should this new leisure time be spent?

Some Jews, particularly rich, long-term urban Jews, followed the Greeks' lead. Ironically, the Jerusalem priesthood—the *Kohanim*, those used to being close to power by virtue of their control over the cult of the Temple, including the all-important sacrifices and holidays, and responsible for the official national image of the Jewish religion—were among the leading Hellenizers, as these nouveau Greeks were called. They believed that leisure time should be used for pleasure. They worshipped Nike, Puma, Adidas and other pagan gods.

Other Jews, called the *Ḥasidim* (no relation to the Brooklyn kind), felt that free time should be used to study Torah, to come closer to God, and to make the world a better place for all to live in peace and prosperity. They saw this educational ethos as a religious process and not merely an examination of scientific, social and political realities. These were Ezra the Scribe's spiritual children, and their process of weekly Torah reading had bonded them into a tight community. Much of their leadership came from the rural priesthood.

As cities grew, synagogues evolved as important places where groups of Jews gathered regularly to worship. Families often shared courtyards with other families. Sometimes they formed *ḥavurot*, special fellowship groups, in order to celebrate Shabbat properly, carefully follow the laws of tithing, and observe other Jewish customs. The *Beit Midrash*, the House of Study, became another one of their important institutions. Here, when they gathered to study Torah, a Jewish leisure-time activity, people would share customs and practices from their home villages. They would compare the ways their town elders interpreted and adapted the law. Discussions about how best to understand and follow the Torah became important. In the cities, empowered by proximity and leisure time, the roots of a new Judaism were growing—as were the tentacles of Greek culture and assimilation.

A NOTE ON HISTORICITY

The key premise of this introduction is that the conditions which contributed to The Ever-Evolving Story of Ḥanukkah involved dramatic economic and social change in Judea. This can be seen most clearly in the role of olive oil. If we look at the Talmud *Shabbat 21b-24b,* we see a number of passages which describe Ḥanukkah practice.

> Our rabbis taught: The mitzvah of Ḥanukkah is for each family to light one lamp. The one who wishes to beautify this mitzvah fully should light one lamp for each person in the family. The one who wishes to beautify

this mitzvah completely—*Beit* Shammai taught that one should light eight lights on the first night, and one less each following day. *Beit* Hillel taught that one should light one light on the first day and one more each following day...

One cannot use the Hanukkah lamp for personal needs; for that, one must have an additional lamp. If, however, one has kindled a torch as a Hanukkah lamp, no additional lamp is required...

If one has only enough money for either lighting the Shabbat candles or to kindle the Hanukkah lamp, one should kindle the Shabbat lamp because it brings peace into a household. However, if one must choose between wine for Kiddush and oil for the Hanukkah lamp, one should kindle the Hanukkah lamp because it is more important to publicize the miracle.

The events commemorated by Hanukkah took place around 165 B.C.E. These texts come from the Babylonian Talmud, a document which was assembled between 300 and 500 C.E. This material, which is introduced as *b'raitot*, was clearly assembled after 200 C.E., but may have some connection to conversations which took place as early as 100 B.C.E. There is no easy way to precisely date it, or to exactly pinpoint the social climate it is suggesting. If, however, it does reflect thinking from the time of *Beit* Hillel and *Beit* Shammai, as it claims to, it provides us with an important window on changes which were occurring.

   Read these passages and you will see signs of economic change. On one hand, there is a sense that oil is a very expensive commodity. Some people may not be able to afford any, so special provisions are made to enable them to buy just a very little. There is a sense that one lamp per night, eight nights' worth of oil, is a reasonable expectation for an ordinary Jewish home. On the other hand, both Hillel's and Shammai's schools (middle-class gathering places) see the ideal celebration of Hanukkah involving forty-four lamps full per family member. The gap is astounding, especially since the gap between the practice of the schools of Hillel and Shammai can often be seen as reflecting economic issues, with Hillel defending the less costly practice. Here, they both use the same amount of oil—forty-four or more lamps full—with no apparent concern about cost. While these divergent rulings may reflect a society with radically disproportionate wealth, it is far more likely that they are an historically layered series of rulings, reflecting the growing affordability of light after dark. Remember, for Hillel's and Shammai's schools, Hanukkah was a minor event, as important to them (as a time to spend money on a celebration) as Columbus Day is to us.

ACT TWO: CHAMBER OF HORAS

Now let's see how this economic backdrop affects the politics of the period. Let's do the history by the numbers.

1

Alexander dies in 323 B.C.E. He leaves no successor and soon his kingdom is split up among his leading generals' families. The Middle East is split between two families. The Seleucid family rules the eastern side from Syria, while the Ptolemy family rules the western side from Egypt. For the sake of context, know that Antiochus (whom we will soon meet) is a Seleucid, while Cleopatra (whom we won't meet in this chapter) is a Ptolemy. Judea is in the middle. The Jews there still pay taxes, and life goes on.

2

In the year 200 B.C.E., the Seleucid family wins control of Judea from the Ptolemies. (Remember: No matter who was in charge, Egypt and her playmates were always fighting for control of Judea). For the Judeans, things don't change much. People still pay their taxes and life still goes on.

3

Antiochus III, the Seleucid who took over Judea from the Ptolemies, dies and leaves two sons: Seleucus IV and Antiochus IV, our Antiochus. Seleucus IV dies somewhat mysteriously and Antiochus IV, our villain, takes over his half of the known world. Antiochus IV is relatively mad, seeing himself as a god. Now, it is not unusual for a monarch to see himself as a god, but Antiochus was a little more serious about this than most. He made a point of having himself called Antiochus *Epiphanes* (which means "God Manifest.") His subjects made a point of calling him Antiochus *Epimanes* ("the madman").

4

In a desire to solidify his empire, Antiochus helps Jason, an upstart contender for the Jewish High Priesthood, to unseat the extant High *Kohein*, Onais III. We can assume that Antiochus was well paid for this favor. (Consider the implications of the leading religious Jew in the world being named after a Greek cultural hero.) Under Jason, the city of Jerusalem is officially established as a Greek *polis* (city-state) and renamed "Antiochia." As part of the process, a gymnasium is established and supported by the *Kohanim*.

Imagine all kinds of little future Temple priests running around, attending a naked discus practice while they were supposed to be at Hebrew school. Imagine our Maccabean chorus whispering: "Beware of Greeks baring gifts."

At this point, the *Hasidim* are not at all happy, but people are still paying their taxes and life continues to go on.

5

Just before going to war with the Ptolemies, Antiochus takes a bribe from Menelaus, an even more assimilated contender for the High Priesthood. Antiochus takes the money and tells Jason, "It's not your night, Kid," and then gives Menelaus the title. The Hellenizers are happy. The *Hasidim* are unhappy. But, Antiochus IV is very happy, because Menelaus' bribe allows him to raid the Temple treasury for gold to finance his upcoming campaign to capture a larger portion of the known world.

6

Three things now happen at once. One: Jason, probably backed by the Ptolemies, makes a sudden return and again challenges Menelaus for the title. Two: Angered by the removal of sacred gold objects from the temple—a clearly sacrilegious act—the *Hasidim* are rapidly reaching their boiling point. Three: A rumor of Antiochus' death (probably devised by Antiochus IV, himself) spreads through Judea. Angered by the profanation of the Temple, (ironically) encouraged by Jason's return, and convinced by the rumor that the time is right, the *Hasidim* revolt against Menelaus and the Hellenizing ruling class. Here is where the Hanukkah War really starts—as a religious civil war between two Jewish factions, not as a revolt for freedom.

7

Surprise! Surprise! Surprise! Antiochus isn't dead! He sends in the troops and stops the civil war. In order to quiet things down (so he'll have time to conquer the Ptolemies), he passes a series of prohibitions. He makes a number of basic Jewish practices illegal, among them Shabbat and circumcision. Simultaneously, he begins to demonstrate his authority by forcing local Jewish populations to eat pork publicly and to participate in pagan rites (which probably included worship of our little Mad Manifest god).

A NOTE ON HISTORICITY

Again, before we finish this second part of our Ḥanukkah exploration, let's stop and check the sources.

In the *Second Book of Maccabees* 4:7ff, a book written in Greek, probably around 120 B.C.E. (forty years after the event), we find this account. (The *Second Book of Maccabees* was probably written as a polemic to encourage the large Jewish community living in Egypt to join in the celebration of Ḥanukkah.):

> After Seleucus died, Antiochus, called Epiphanes, ascended the throne. Jason, brother of Onias the High Priest supplanted his brother by promising the King three-hundred and sixty talents of silver and eighty talents from other sources. In addition, he was promised another fifty if he was given permission to build a gymnasium and change the name of the city of Jerusalem to Antiochia. The king agreed and Jason took over. He immediately started to convert his countrymen to the Greek way of life. He broke down the traditional way of life and introduced new customs forbidden by the law. He set up the gymnasium right in the Temple Citadel and introduced the finest young men to the wearing of the Petsus hat (athelete's headgear). The passion for adopting Greek customs rose to such heights that the priests would neglect their Temple service in favor of unlawful exercise, running from their duties as soon as a call came for discus throwing.

While this is clearly not an objective source—all history being written by the victors or by their sponsors—it does clearly show the origins of the Maccabean conflict as a "civil" problem, Jewish factions competing for control of national religious practice. At the same time, this struggle is complicated by the presence of an external monarch who needs money.

In the *First Book of Maccabees*, a Hebrew book written for Judean consumption, we find this account:

> ...then the King (after the revolt by the *Ḥasidim*) ordered all his kingdom to become one people and decreed that everyone should forsake his own law. All of the nations agreed to the decree of the King and sacrificed to idols and violated the Shabbat. The King also sent letters to Jerusalem and to the cities of Judea, commanding them to follow foreign customs, to stop the Temple sacrifices, to violate Shabbat and holidays, to profane the Temple sanctuary, to build high places and...idols, to sacrifice swine flesh and unkosher animals, and to leave their sons uncircumcised...Whoever would not obey the king's orders was to die.

Nevertheless, many Jews were firmly committed not to eat unkosher food. They chose to die rather than defile themselves by food or break the laws of the Covenant. Great was the wrath which was brought upon Israel.

This source, too, is not objective. It clearly carries the thrill of Maccabean victory in every clause. It does, however, show us a progression. What starts out as an internal conflict, a civil war between Hellenizer and *Hasid*, rapidly becomes a rebellion against a foreign ruler. Ironically, this text sees some rationale in Antiochus' actions. It senses that his imposition of religion may not have been a crazed act, but a universal policy designed at ending differences (and stopping his own miniature version of Pakistan-India, Northern Ireland, etc.). The text understands, however, that homogeneity is not a realistic solution and essentially says: "So, on with the revolution."

ACT THREE: OIL'S WELL THAT ENDS WELL

Let's do a bit of *Judas Maccabeus*, the Handel oratorio, and tell the epic part of the tale. One of my favorite pieces of Americana is the fact that John Belushi once played Judah "The Hammer" Maccabee in a "Saturday Night Live" sketch—and he did it more or less straight. There were no jokes. Simply, every time his name was said, the rest of the cast would become a chorus and fill "The Hammer" into a gap between "Judah" and "Maccabee." Otherwise, it was just a dramatic recreation of the basic childhood version—Judah Maccabee as a combination of William Tell and Robin Hood. Essentially, Handel's version, Belushi's version, the preserved "authentic myth," goes like this:

Antiochus IV decides that he has had enough of the Jewish religion. To make sure, he puts a show on the road. And so, to every village and hamlet his soldiers go, bringing his idol, his recipe for cream-o-pork stew, his laws, and his way of life. You may ask at this point, "Why a road show? Why not just disseminate the decrees from Antiochia (a.k.a. Jerusalem)?" The answer goes back to our socioeconomic origins. The Hellenizers were rich city kids, led by rich city priests. The *Hasidim* were rural kids who moved to the cities to get better jobs. Their leaders were rural priests. Unlike the simple picture of the children of Aaron all gathering annually for the Priesthood Annual Picnic and Photo Opportunity which is often learned in Sunday School, competitive groups and classes of priests were always struggling for power. If you wanted to stamp out the *Hasidic* Rebellion, you had to get at its roots, the small priestly towns.

Modi'in was one such town. Among its priestly inhabitants was a family known as *Hashmon*, including Mattathias and his kids. (According to some historians, Mattathias and family had been part of the priestly hierarchy in Jerusalem but escaped to the rural areas to plan their anti-Hellenistic rebellion.) Antiochus' soldiers come to town, set up their idol, and/or their cream-o-pork stew (depending on the version)—and order everyone upon penalty of death to bow down, eat, or both. One Jew gives in. Suddenly, a short sword emerges from underneath a cloak. The Jewish apostate falls dead. Mattathias, a town leader, shouts "All who are for the Lord follow me." And chaos erupts. Within an instant the Syrian soldiers are dead and the Hashmon family flees to the hills. (According to an *aggadah*—legend—they were singing Moses and Miriam's old battle hymn: *"Mi khamokha ba'eilim Adonai,* Who is like You, Adonai, among the other gods?" (Exodus 15:11) One version says that M a C a B E comes from the first letters of these words. Another version says that Maccabee means "a hammer." Somehow, the Hasmonean guerilla army becomes the Maccabees (not a Liberation Front).

Our heroes fight a guerilla war against the Syrians (a.k.a. the house of Seleucid) and drive them out of Judea. Early in the process Mattathias dies, and young Judah takes over, continuing to fight the good fight. Eventually, they take the Temple, clean it out, rebuild the altar and do something to rededicate the Temple—exactly what remains a mystery. Later, the date of this rededication, the 25th of Kislev, becomes the beginning of a national holiday celebrated for eight days, involving special lights and the saying of Hallel. Here are the four possibilities.

Ending One: *I Maccabees* 4:39-59

> They purified the Temple, removed the stones which defiled it...they took unhewed stones, as the law commands, and built a new altar on the model of the old one. They rebuilt the Sanctuary and restored its interior and courts. They fixed the sacred vessels and menorah. When they had the Shew Bread on the Table and had hung the curtains, and all their work was complete, then early on the twenty-fifth day of the month of Kislev...it was rededicated with hymns of thanksgiving...Then Judah, his brothers, and the whole congregation of Israel decreed that the rededication of the altar should be observed with joy and gladness at the same time each year.

As we learned earlier, the *First Book of Maccabees* was probably written in Hebrew in Judah around 120 B.C.E., forty-five years after the first Hanukkah. It is the non-eyewitness account which is closest to the actual events. When we read it we see some important details: (a) the date, (b) the details of cleaning and rededication of the Temple, (c) the rekindling of the lights, (d) the saying of psalms of praise (a form of Hallel), and (e) the creation of an annual observance. What is missing is any sense of miracle. That is: they came, they cleaned, they dedicated. The version of the Hanukkah story found in the *Jewish Antiquities* by Flavius Josephus (circa 93-94 C.E.) is a virtual gloss of this text. It presents an identical history and an identical set of details.

Ending Two: *II Maccabees* 10:1-8

Recall that *Second Maccabees* was written in Greek and was designed to encourage Egyptian Jewry, particularly the large population in Alexandria, to adopt the observance of Hanukkah. Here the account of the dedication of the Temple shares lots of details, but offers a whole new twist.

> Maccabeus with his men, led by the Lord, recovered the Temple and the city of Jerusalem. He demolished the altars erected by the heathens in the public square and their sacred precincts as well. When they had purified the sanctuary, they constructed another altar, then striking fire from flints, they offered the lights, and the Shew Bread...The sanctuary was purified on the twenty-fifth day of Kislev...This joyful celebration went on for eight days, it was like Sukkot, for they recalled how only a short time before they had kept the festival while living like animals in the mountains, and so they carried *lulavim* and *etrogim*, and they chanted hymns to God who had triumphantly led them to the purification of the Temple. A measure was passed by the public assembly that the entire Jewish people should observe these days every year.

Once more, the key details are all mentioned: (a) the date, (b) the details of cleaning and rededication of the Temple, (c) the rekindling of the lights, (d) the saying of hymns (psalms of praise), and (e) the creation of an annual observance. Two important elements have been added. First, we are now told that Hanukkah is an eight-day celebration. Second, we are told that Hanukkah began as a second celebration of the eight-day Sukkot holiday.

Ending Three: *Pesikta Rabbati*

Pesikta Rabbati is a collection of *midrashim* and other rabbinic odds and ends put together in the Land of Israel at more or less the same time that the Babylonian rabbinate was organizing, debating, collecting and redacting the Talmud. In other words, post-200 C.E. Notice that it contains the key elements of (a) the date, (b) the kindling of the lights, (c) the saying of Hallel, and (d) the "eightness" of the celebration. Missing here are the details of the clean-up and the creation of an annual observance. Both of these are relatively unnecessary, because by the date of *Pesikta Rabbati's* creation, these were assumed facts.

Why are lights kindled during Ḥanukkah?

At the time the sons of *Hashmon* triumphed over the kingdom of Greece, they entered the Temple and they found there eight spears of iron which they grooved out, poured in oil, and kindled wicks.

Why is the Hallel read?

Because Hallel is not read except on the overthrow of a kingdom, and since the kingdom of Antiochus continued, Hallel was not said at that time but since the kingdom of Greece was destroyed, Hallel is now said...Saying: "In times past we were servants to Pharaoh and to Greece; but now we are servants to the Holy One. 'O servants of the Lord, give praise'" (Psalm 113).

This text is clearly designed to answer three questions: (1) Why do we light Ḥanukkah lights?, (2) Why do we celebrate for eight nights?, and (3) Why do we say Hallel? These Israel-based answers are all military. They all have to do with the military victory (which they attribute to God—not to the Maccabees).

Ending Four: The Babylonian Talmud, *Shabbat 21b*

By contrast, this account from the Babylonian Talmud (which we read at the beginning of this chapter), answers the same three questions: (1) Why do we light Ḥanukkah lights?, (2) Why do we celebrate for eight nights?, and (3) Why do we say Hallel? While the Israel-based answers are all military in nature, albeit emphasizing God's role in the victory, this Babylonian version still relies on God but eliminates the victory. In giving the solution, the "miracle of the oil" now acts as a replacement for military aspects found elsewhere.

> Our rabbis taught: On the twenty-fifth of Kislev begins the eight days of Ḥanukkah, which are days on which mourning and fasting are prohibited.
>
> For, when the Greeks entered the Temple, they defiled all of the oil; and when the Hasmonean dynasty defeated them, they searched and found only one jug of oil with the official seal of the Head *Kohein*, enough to burn for one day. But a miracle happened and the oil lasted for eight days.
>
> In the following years, these days were appointed as a festival on which Hallel was said.

In the Babylonian Talmud, there is no residue of conflict. There is no sense of war or fighting—that has all moved "off camera" into the background. The focus is no longer victory or even human rededication, but rather Divine intervention. The message of Hanukkah has now been carefully rewritten to the key line in the rabbinically assigned Haftorah portion, Zekhariah 4:6, "Not by might and not by power, but by My spirit alone, says Adonai." Like the Haggadah's reworking of the Exodus from Egypt (redemption comes from God's involvement, not human action—Moses does not appear), the rabbis remove Judah & Co. from the chain of causality. In his place, the single pitcher of holy oil burns brightly.

Ironically, this last writing down of Hanukkah has completely inverted the meaning found in the first written version. In the *First Book of Maccabees*, God is never mentioned. Here, God has become the whole story.

A RECONSTRUCTION

"Reconstruction" is a word historians use a lot. The writing of history is essentially the evolution of a subjective viewpoint extrapolated from a lot of earlier subjective viewpoints. History is made up of best guesses.

There is no longer a way of knowing the absolute "true" story of Hanukkah, but there are ways of taking very good guesses.

Life in the land of Israel was drastically different after the return from the Babylonian Exile than it was before. A new sense of a local rather than national religious process was making an appearance. The roots of Torah-centered, synagogue Judaism had now been planted and were beginning to sprout.

The presence of Alexander the Great, two hundred years later, supercharged this process of change. Economic opportunities and cultural diversity changed the fabric of daily life. The presence of outside political influences allowed the possibility of intrigue. As the first elements of a proto-rabbinic Judaism began to germinate in this new climate, they were immediately drawn into a social and political struggle against the assimilationist tendencies compelled by Greek culture. The conflict, which began as a social struggle over the best way to spend leisure time (and the meaning of education), became a political struggle over the control of the symbol of national worship, the High Priesthood. This political struggle escalated into a civil war, which in turn (in ways similar to many such wars in our day and age), came to involve the army of an outside power and became a full-scale war—a revolution against a colonial authority.

The short-term end result was a guerilla victory which became the paradigmatic model for continuing struggles for national liberation. The Hasmoneans quickly took local power as kings and priests. But, within a generation, they had transferred ultimate authority back to the Seleucid Emperors who were now more respectful of their illusion of autonomy. Taxes were paid and business went on in their Kingdom as usual. The pattern continued until Rome entered the scene and again upped the stakes (literally and symbolically). But that story leads to a different religion's winter solstice celebration.

It's probable that the 25th of Kislev, or thereabouts, was always a local fire-lighting holiday. Such a celebration is found in almost every culture. As the days get shorter, and the sun seems to be going away, conventional wisdom in a preastronomical mind teaches that you light your own fires in order to encourage its return. You learn that in "Symbolic Magic 101." That's why our neighbors put up electrically burning trees at the same time of year. It's a questions of orbits, not coincidence. Therefore, it's likely that when the Maccabees won a winter solstice victory and rededicated the Temple, the celebration got linked to fire. (Think about it—Hanukkah wouldn't work anywhere near as well if you celebrated around July 21st in Northern Finland.)

It's likely that the first Hanukkah celebration—that first rededication—functioned as a "make-up" Sukkot, just as the *Second Book of Maccabees* suggests. In those days, Sukkot was one of the most important popular holidays of the year. Yom Kippur was essentially for priests—their way of getting clean, pure and holy for Sukkot, the real public event. It was Sukkot which began the rainy season, and it was Sukkot which included the petitions for rain. The idea of a "second" Sukkot isn't far-fetched. In the Torah we find provisions for a "second Passover" which is celebrated later by those who were traveling and missed the first one. This second Sukkot falls into the same category.

Hanukkah as Sukkot explains a lot of things. It gives us eight days, because Sukkot was an eight-day holiday (counting Shemini Atzeret). It gives us Hallel (even without an active Divine intervention) because Hallel is said on each pilgrimage festival, Sukkot included. And, it gives us a sense of the dedication of the original Temple.

Even in the Babylonian Talmud, the last and most varied of these sources, we see a clue to the Sukkot connection. In a passage we looked at earlier, *Beit* Hillel and *Beit* Shammai argue over the pattern of candlelighting on Hanukkah (8-7-6-5-4-3-2-1 vs. 1-2-3-4-5-6-7-8).

> Our rabbis taught: The mitzvah of Hanukkah is for each family to light one lamp. The one who wishes to beautify this mitzvah fully, should light one lamp for each person in the family. The one who wishes to beautify this mitzvah completely—*Beit* Shammai taught that one should light eight lights on the first night, and one less each following day. *Beit* Hillel taught that one should light one light on the first night and one more each following day...

> In Palestine, two *amorim* (teachers) explained their position: Rabbi Yose ben Abin and Rabbi Yose ben Zabida. One taught: *Beit* Shammai's reason corresponds to the days to come (in the holiday), while *Beit* Hillel's reason corresponds to the days which have passed. The other taught: *Beit* Shammai's reason corresponds to the descending order of

the cattle sacrificed on Sukkot. *Beit* Hillel's reason was that we ascend in the matters of holiness and do not descend.

Shabbat 21b ff.

Our clue is found in *Beit* Shammai's reason according to Rabbi Yose ben Zabida: "*Beit* Shammai's reason corresponds to the descending order of the cattle sacrificed on Sukkot." In the Torah we find a description of the special Sukkot sacrifices, eight bullocks the first day, seven the second, etc. Seemingly, *Beit* Shammai's memory of reasons for Hanukkah customs goes back to a primordial memory of Sukkot.

Within a generation, Hanukkah was no longer a second Sukkot. In the Land of Israel, the new Hasmonean state was in power, and Hanukkah could easily be seen as a celebration of national liberation. It no longer had to rest on an earlier religious custom (any more than the modern state of Israel would connect Yom Ha-Atsmaut [Israeli Independence Day] to Shavuot [The Feast of Weeks].) By the time the *First Book of Maccabees* was written, the original Sukkot connection had probably become irrelevant. The same was not true in Egypt, where a powerful religious rather than political component was needed to motivate the practice. Therefore, the author probably trucked out the old Sukkot memory and put it to good use.

When the calendar switches to the Talmudic era (some three to four hundred years later), the world is a very different place. The Land of Israel has experienced a series of holocausts at the hands of the Romans in which whole generations rebelled and were wiped out. The Second Temple has been long since destroyed. Jerusalem has been burned, torn down stone by stone, and the soil sown with salt so that nothing would grow.

The Judaism which survived did so primarily in the midst of another foreign empire, Persia. Obedience was the key to Jewish survival and prosperity there. Jews were able to "do well" if they "didn't rock the boat." The last thing the politicians and merchants who patronized the *yeshivot* (schools) wanted was to have children told the stories of brave soldiers who fought to the death for Jewish freedom and Jewish Independence. For them, the Jewish way was faith in God, accommodation, and really good negotiating teams always working behind the scenes. It was a time and a place where a long-lasting jug of holy oil illuminated more than the sling and the sword. So, as with every other generation, their Hanukkah story became a way of meeting their own perceived needs by giving it a slant meaningful to them.

Meanwhile, back in the Land of Israel, rabbinic life was by-and-large limited to a few cities in the Galilee. Living again as farmers, fishermen, or as craftsmen in small villages, the Judean rabbis continued their study and their teaching quietly. But, unlike their Babylonian colleagues who lived comfortably within the economic well-being of a prosperous foreign land, the Judean rabbis eked out a living within the ruined shell of what had once been Jewish civilization. For them, the past was much more recent, the future much more necessary. Their version of the Hanukkah story—that eight spears became torches—and the knowledge that the Greek Empire was eventually defeated, plays off a quiet, messianic hope that a new generation of Maccabees would again reestablish and rededicate Jewish life.

ULTIMATE MEANING

On the wall of my office is a wonderful Barton's Chocolate booklet from 1950. It is called "The Story of Chanukah—New Dreidle Games." It tells the Hanukkah story in a series of cartoon panels this way:

1. 169 B.C.E. Judea was under the rule of the Cruel Syrian King Antiochus.

2. There was no organized opposition except for occasional guerilla attacks on the King's soldiers.

Notice, Antiochus has become "cruel" and the band of merry men are already in Sherwood Forest doing the "guerilla thing"—just waiting for Judah to organize them.

3. Mattathias, the Hasmonean, High Priest of Modi'in, and his five sons rallied the Jewish people and formed a small army.

Notice three things: Mattathias has become a High Priest of a small town—a complete impossibility. Only Jerusalem had a High Priest, elsewhere there were leading priests. But in this rewrite, as in many "lost prince" stories, a lost throne empowers Mattathias and company to win the war and "regain power."

Second, the Syrian cruelty no longer involves religious oppression. The "idol" and the "forced *treif* (unkosher) eating" have been completely removed. We are now talking about "political freedom" from a "cruel king," not "not eating pork." In Barton's vision of their audience, pork isn't worth dying over, neither are idols—but "FREEDOM" is!!!

Third, we instantly grant Mattathias credit for a small army (making him a national liberation front—one the USA could fund, as opposed to an "unorganized" rebel guerilla, whom our government could not fund.) In this Hanukkah reality, bureaucracy has become a virtue. Mattathias' big contribution in Barton's Hanukkah reality is not faith, but organizational skills.

If you read closely, and think about 1950, this is Hanukkah as the Korean War! This is a small group of "well-organized" rightful leaders who are using guerilla tactics to win back authority and bring their rightful government back from exile—religion is not involved, except as a national symbol. Their narrative continues for four more panels in a similar way.

4.   In 167 B.C.E., after many spectacular victories over the enemy, Mattathias died and his son Judah, the Maccabee, assumed command.

5.   Under Judah, the greatly outnumbered Jewish army liberated most of Judea. Then, through a clever strategic maneuver, they routed Antiochus' mightiest army before Jerusalem, the site of the Holy Temple.

6.   On the 25th of Kislev, 165, the Jewish Army marched into Jerusalem and rededicated the Temple. Chanukah means dedication.

And if you read carefully, you will notice that this chocolate-covered Temple was never desecrated by pagans and never cleansed and rebuilt by Jews—it just had a new dedication ceremony. If you read this story in its own context (and forget the other versions you know), dedication now means commitment. Judah and his well-organized, strategic army were dedicated, too. Dedication in this story means "All-American commitment."

7.   Only one small jar of holy oil was found. However, the Menorah miraculously burned eight days during which clean oil was made. We therefore celebrate Chanukah eight days.

In Barton's Jewish world, the High Priest has vanished. Holy means "clean"—the oil has no sense of being set apart, as the term "holy" really means; it is just "clean oil" for Barton's. In the end, there is a miracle, but it has no source or purpose.

   The Barton's Ḥanukkah myth is the story of a band of rightful leaders who organize an army and win their liberation through dedication and strategy. The miracle of the oil story exists as a tag, a memory separated from the psuedo-historic precision of a myth which has the good sense to use B.C.E. While glorifying the Maccabees, holiness has become meaningless and separate from the real reason for the conflict: "Jews Suffered Greatly." Here, the religious is blatantly a public cover for the real issue: liberation.
   In their remaining two panels, Bartonic sages tell us the history of the dreidle:

8.   When Antiochus forbade the study of Torah, Jews gathered secretly in the woods and studied by heart, with a woman as lookout.

9.   When warned of approaching soldiers, they would spin a four-sided dreidle, a favorite game of Judah's men.

This is a wonderful modern midrash (creative exercise). It has all the markings of a World War II spy tale, or more accurately a gangster movie. Women lookouts and men playing dice as a cover to a secret meeting is James Cagney stuff. As we will learn, the dreidle was actually a Ḥanukkah innovation evolved in medieval Germany.

Every Hanukkah we stand with our families by the *hanukkiyah*, as every generation since the first has done, and we perform the prescribed ritual of blessings and songs. Then, we are left to tell the story on our own. In each of our tellings, we meet many Maccabees and many miracles, for each generation tells the tale out of its collective wisdom, and out of what they have personally come to understand. In the glow of the flames, the original heroism and the original miracle is continually recreated and rededicated.

WOMEN AND HANUKKAH

The *Shulhan Arukh*, the Code of Jewish Law, specifies that while the Hanukkah lights are burning, no one is to engage in work, especially women. Why women? There are two famous stories of Hanukkah that have brought special merit to the valorous role of women in the holiday.

JUDITH AND HOLOFERNES

The Apocrypha is a collection of books from the biblical period which were not chosen to be part of the Jewish Bible (but were accepted in the Catholic collection). In addition to the *First and Second Books of Maccabees,* the Apocrypha contains the *Book of Judith*, a book preserved in the Greek but not in the Hebrew Bible. It tells the story of a beautiful Jewish woman by the name of Judith who single-handedly saved the Jewish town of Bethulia during the Hasmonean Revolt.

The story goes like this. An evil general, Holofernes, lays siege to the town. All seems lost until Judith tells the Elders of the town that she has a plan to defeat the enemy. They dismiss her offer as foolish and prepare to surrender to Holofernes. Judith tries once more to convince the Elders that she can save them, and this time they reluctantly agree to allow her to leave the camp for one day.

Judith prepares herself for her bold scheme. She dresses provocatively and prepares a sack containing food and wine. She approaches the enemy camp and is immediately captured and brought to Holofernes. He is very impressed with her beauty and her prediction that he will capture Bethulia. She suggests they go to his tent alone and celebrate.

Once in Holofernes' tent, Judith feeds him the salty cheese she has brought with her. Holofernes becomes quite thirsty and drinks large quantities of wine until he falls asleep drunk. Judith takes Holofernes' sword and cuts off his head. She covers the body with a blanket, puts the head in a sack, and returns through the sleeping camp to Bethulia.

The Elders cannot believe that Judith has returned safely. She reveals the severed head of Holofernes and the Elders place it on the walls of the city. Meanwhile, the enemy soldiers awake and discover the decapitated body of their leader. In the distance, they see

Holofernes' head hanging from the walls of Bethulia. They decide that if a Jewish woman could be so ruthless, they do not want to fight Jewish men in battle, and so the army retreats and the city of Bethulia is saved.

A midrash (in Hebrew) dealing with a variation of the Judith story was read on the Shabbat or *Shabbatot* of Hanukkah during the Middle Ages. Dated sometime after the 10th century C.E., the midrash is remarkably similar to the narrative of the Greek version (see Bernard H. Mehlman and Daniel F. Polish, "A Midrash for Hanukkah," *Conservative Judaism*, Vol. 36 (2), Winter, 1982).

Artist and critic Beth Haber notes that the story of Judith has inspired a long list of artistic representations, ranging from the rather violent depictions of the beheading of Holofernes by Andrea Mantegna to the stone sculptures of Judith on the north portal wall of the Chartres Cathedral. Michelangelo himself painted figures of Judith and her maid on the Sistine Chapel ceiling. Elisabetta Sirani and Fede Galizia used Judith as subject, while Carravaggio's famous painting is far more sympathetic to Holofernes than to Judith. A series of six paintings by Artemesia Gentileschi runs the gamut from the violence of the act itself to the resolve and determination in its aftermath. In addition, the Judith story also inspired a number of religious epics in many European countries, as well as musical oratorios by famous and not-so-famous composers.

HANNAH AND HER SONS

Another story of heroism involving a woman is associated with Hanukkah. The story of Hannah and her seven sons is recorded in the *Second Book of Maccabees* 7:1-41. Unlike the militant story of Judith, Hannah's story is a tale of martyrdom. It seems that Antiochus meets Hannah and her sons who refuse to eat pig in public. As each son refuses, he is tortured and put to death in front of Hannah. Finally, before the last child is to be killed, Antiochus appeals to Hannah to direct him to eat the meat and be saved. Hannah asks her son what he wishes to do. He replies that he is only sorry that he had to wait so long to show his love of Torah. Hannah praises him and he is then martyred. Hannah dies, too. In different versions, Hannah is killed by Antiochus, throws herself from the city walls, or dies of grief over her beloved sons.

These stories of heroism shed light on the role of Jewish women in times of crisis. From the time of the Israelite midwives' refusal to accede to Pharaoh's decree to kill the firstborn Jewish males (see Exodus 1:15-22) to the leadership of Deborah (Judges 4 and 5), the Jewish woman understands the severity of the situation and rallies the Jewish people to victory. In the Judith story, the Israelite men are depicted as weak and indecisive while she is willing to risk her own life to turn the tide.

3

The H̲anukkah Ritual

I always got a new doll. Oh, the smell of the plastic and flannel. I think a Barbie Doll or Betsy Wetsy or one of those. The smell is what I remember.

Beverly Weise

My earliest memory is that my sister and I fought over who would get the family *h̲anukkiyah* that plays "Hatikvah." When you light the candles, you turn it on and it plays "Hatikvah." My sister got "Hatikvah" and I got the Seder plate. That is what I remember.

Janice Reznik

Open up a traditional prayerbook and look at the Hebrew index and you will find the words *Seder Hanukkah*, the "Order of Hanukkah." Like every other Jewish ritual, the Hanukkah candlelighting has a fixed order and choreography, what is known in Hebrew as a *seder*, a progression, and what in English we might awkwardly label a "Table Service."

The idea of a "seder" is of course best known from Passover, where a progression of fifteen steps shapes a complicated process which allows us to relive and reexperience the Exodus from Egypt. In the same way, we are used to daily and Shabbat services flowing through a fixed progression of prayers found in the *siddur* (from the same root as *seder*). Even the way we conjure and welcome Shabbat into our homes every Friday night follows a fixed pattern of prayers and actions. (That is why we called the first volume in The Art of Jewish Living series, *The Shabbat Seder.*)

The Hanukkah ritual is too short to call it a seder, yet, it has a fixed order of blessings and a fixed progression of actions. This progression takes us through a process. Think of it as one of the rides at Disney World where you get into a car that rolls or floats on a track. The ride takes you through a process: You encounter one experience, then the next, then the next. The order is always fixed, the experience cumulative. Each blessing and each prayer in the Hanukkah candlelighting service has a purpose and a function in bringing the religious experience of Hanukkah alive.

The basic Hanukkah "kindling service" consists of three *b'rakhot* (blessings) on the first night (two on the next seven nights) and then two song/prayers.

1.   First, we say the mitzvah *b'rakhah* "*L'hadlik ner shel Hanukkah.*" This defines the act of lighting the Hanukkah lights as a "mitzvah," a commanded religious experience, and establishes an expectation that this act can lead (if we have the proper intention) to an encounter with the Divine.

2.   Next, we say a *b'rakhah* of praise,"*Sheh'asah nissim la'avoteinu.*" This *b'rakhah* not only thanks God for the original Hanukkah experience that we are now recalling, but defines Hanukkah as the commemoration of a time when God performed miracles. In other words, this one line *b'rakhah* teaches us Hanukkah's essential meaning (as expressed by the rabbis): "Not by might, not by power, but by My spirit alone, says the Lord." In other words, we are clearly taught that Hanukkah is the acknowledgement of God's actions on our behalf.

3. As our final *b'rakhah* (and only on the first night) we say the "*Shehehheyanu.*" This blessing is said at the beginning of every major Jewish religious experience. It acknowledges our entry into a special time, a holy time. But in a real sense, *Shehehheyanu* is a connector. Its words thank God for "continuing our life," "continuing our establishment," and "bringing us along." In short, it is a blessing for growth and continuity. When we say it, we establish a link between the moment we are experiencing and the core of our life. It expresses the hope that this moment's meaning will further enrich the meaning of every experience which has led us here, and help to sharpen our sense of direction from here on. As the last expression of blessing on the first eve of the mitzvah, *Shehehheyanu* is a call for connection and significance.

4. *Ha-neirot Hallalu* is a short prayer written in the Gaonic period (after the Talmud was finished). It is a kind of instant Hanukkah lesson, one which reviews all the key points expressed in the Talmud. *Ha-neirot Hallalu* is a kind of miniature "Hanukkah Haggadah," a one paragraph authorized explanation of the Hanukkah story.

5. *Maoz Tzur* is a medieval song which further thanks God for the miracle of Divine intervention. It continues the themes begun in *Sheh'asah nissim la'avoteinu* (# 2.)and expanded in *Ha-neirot Hallalu* (# 4.). It seals the Hanukkah ritual experience with a call upon God to work future redemptions, just as God effected an earlier redemption in the time of the Maccabees.

HANUKKAH CHECKLIST

_____ *Hanukkiyah* (at least one per family)

_____ Oil and wicks for eight nights OR

_____ 44 candles

_____ Matches (use long fireplace matches)

_____ .Text of blessings and songs

_____ Dreidle(s)

_____ Hanukkah gelt

_____ *Tzedakah* box

_____ Traditional foods (latkes, *sufganiyot* [doughnuts], and foods cooked in oil)

1

הַדְלָקַת נֵרוֹת   *HADLAKAT NEIROT*
CANDLELIGHTING

בָּרוּךְ אַתָּה יהוה   *Barukh atah Adonai*

אֱלֹהֵינוּ מֶלֶךְ הָעוֹלָם   *Eloheinu melekh ha-olam*

אֲשֶׁר קִדְּשָׁנוּ בְּמִצְוֹתָיו   *Asher kidshanu b'mitzvotav*

וְצִוָּנוּ   *V'tzivanu*

לְהַדְלִיק נֵר שֶׁל חֲנֻכָּה.   *L'hadlik ner shel Hanukkah.*

Praised are You, Adonai,
Our God, Ruler of the universe,
Who made us holy through the commandments
and commanded us
to kindle the Hanukkah lights.

2

שֶׁעָשָׂה נִסִּים *SHEH'ASAH NISSIM*
לַאֲבוֹתֵינוּ *LA'AVOTEINU*

THE ONE WHO DID MIRACLES FOR OUR ANCESTORS

בָּרוּךְ אַתָּה יהוה   *Barukh atah Adonai*

אֱלֹהֵינוּ מֶלֶךְ הָעוֹלָם   *Eloheinu melekh ha-olam,*

שֶׁעָשָׂה נִסִּים לַאֲבוֹתֵינוּ   *Sheh'asah nissim la'avoteinu*

בַּיָּמִים הָהֵם   *Ba-yamim ha-heim*

בַּזְּמַן הַזֶּה.   *Ba-z'man ha-zeh.*

Praised are You, Adonai,
Our God, Ruler of the universe,
Who performed wondrous deeds for our ancestors
in those (ancient) days
at this season.

3

שֶׁהֶחֱיָנוּ *SHEHEHEYANU*

WHO HAS GIVEN US LIFE
(on the first night only:)

בָּרוּךְ אַתָּה יהוה   *Barukh atah Adonai*

אֱלֹהֵינוּ מֶלֶךְ הָעוֹלָם   *Eloheinu melekh ha-olam*

שֶׁהֶחֱיָנוּ   *sheheheyanu*

וְקִיְּמָנוּ   *v'ki-y'manu*

וְהִגִּיעָנוּ   *v'higiyanu*

לַזְּמַן הַזֶּה.   *la-z'man ha-zeh.*

Praised are You, Adonai,
Our God, Ruler of the universe,
Who has given us life
and sustained us
and enabled us to reach
this season.

4

הַנֵּרוֹת הַלָּלוּ *HA-NEIROT HALLALU—* THESE LIGHTS

הַנֵּרוֹת הַלָּלוּ	*Ha-neirot hallalu*
אֲנַחְנוּ מַדְלִיקִין	*Anahnu madlikin*
עַל הַנִּסִּים	*Al ha-nissim*
וְעַל הַנִּפְלָאוֹת	*V'al ha-nif'la-ot*
וְעַל הַתְּשׁוּעוֹת	*V'al ha-t'shu-ot*
וְעַל הַמִּלְחָמוֹת	*V'al ha-mil'ha-mot*
שֶׁעָשִׂיתָ לַאֲבוֹתֵינוּ	*She'asita la-avoteinu*
בַּיָּמִים הָהֵם	*Ba-yamim ha-heim*
בַּזְּמַן הַזֶּה	*Ba-z'man ha-zeh*
עַל יְדֵי כֹּהֲנֶיךָ הַקְּדוֹשִׁים.	*Al y'dei kohanekha ha-k'doshim.*
וְכָל-שְׁמוֹנַת יְמֵי חֲנֻכָּה	*V'khol sh'monat y'mei Hanukkah*
הַנֵּרוֹת הַלָּלוּ קֹדֶשׁ הֵם	*Ha-neirot hallalu kodesh heim,*
וְאֵין לָנוּ רְשׁוּת	*V'ein lanu r'shut*
לְהִשְׁתַּמֵּשׁ בָּהֶם	*L'hishtameish ba-hem*
אֶלָּא לִרְאוֹתָם בִּלְבָד,	*Elah lirotam bilvad,*
כְּדֵי לְהוֹדוֹת וּלְהַלֵּל	*K'dei l'hodot u-l'haleil*
לְשִׁמְךָ הַגָּדוֹל	*L'shimkha ha-gadol*
עַל נִסֶּיךָ וְעַל נִפְלְאוֹתֶיךָ	*Al nisekha v'al nif'l'otekha*
וְעַל יְשׁוּעָתֶךָ.	*V'al y'shu-ah-tekhah.*

These lights
we kindle
(to recall) the miracles
and the wonders
and the deliverance
and the victories (battles)
that our ancestors accomplished
in those days
at this season
through the hands of Your holy priests.
And throughout all eight days of Hanukkah
these lights are sanctified
and we may not
use them
except to look upon them
in order to thank and praise
Your great name
for Your miracles and for Your wonders
and for Your deliverance.

5

מָעוֹז צוּר *MAOZ TZUR—*
ROCK OF AGES

מָעוֹז צוּר יְשׁוּעָתִי	*Maoz tzur y'shu-ah-ti,*
לְךָ נָאֶה לְשַׁבֵּחַ.	*L'kha na-eh l'shabei-ah.*
תִּכּוֹן בֵּית תְּפִלָּתִי	*Tikkon beit t'filati*
וְשָׁם תּוֹדָה נְזַבֵּחַ.	*V'sham todah n'zabei-ah.*
לְעֵת תָּכִין מַטְבֵּחַ	*L'eit takhin mat'bei-ah*
מִצָּר הַמְנַבֵּחַ.	*Mi-tzar ha-m'nabei'ah,*
אָז אֶגְמוֹר בְּשִׁיר מִזְמוֹר	*Az egmor b'shir mizmor*
חֲנֻכַּת הַמִּזְבֵּחַ.	*Hanukkat ha-miz'bei-ah.*

Rock of Ages, let our song praise Your saving power.
You amid the raging throng were our sheltering tower.
Furious they assailed us, but Your help availed us.
And Your word broke their sword when our own strength failed us.

4

הַדְלָקַת נֵרוֹת

HADLAKAT NEIROT
CANDLELIGHTING

ALISSA BOBROW: I remember it was only a few years ago when we first got the dog and he was going by the table with the *ḥanukkiyah* on it and he kept swishing his tail and all the candles were flying all over the place and he was about to catch everything on fire.

YOUR AUTHOR: Oh my, but he didn't, did he?

SHLOMO BOBROW: That would've make some kind of a *shamash*, wouldn't it?

KAREN BOBROW: His name is Freckles.

ALISSA BOBROW: Last year we played dreidle and I lost all of my money and Freckles burned his tail again.

Night has meanings all its own. Darkness, too, elicits strong feelings. Even without context, the words "darkness" and "night" convey much emotion. As these words evoke images, a growing sense of terror and fear intertwines with a sense of peace and rest. Night is a time of love. Night is a time of deep conversations. Night is a time for things that go bump. All the best symbols evoke ambivalent and diffuse feelings.

In the midrash we find an account of the first human night. Adam and Eve spend their first day enjoying God's creations. The world is light and life. Then suddenly, late in the first afternoon, panic sets in. The sun, which had given light and life, turns blood red and starts to sink into oblivion. Suddenly, there is the terror that creation is unraveling, that after only a brief instance, all is coming to an end. Fear of night, fear of darkness, descends into the world. Adam and Eve are coming unglued. Then God becomes manifest, calms them down, and explains that the sun will indeed return. As the darkness grows, God shows them the beauty of the stars and the other night lights. Then, He puts them to bed. In one version, God even braids Eve's hair.

This midrash taps into people's primordial sense of night and darkness: fear and wonder. The same range of emotions plays against the cycle of the seasons. Winter brings not only the cold, but a growing darkness. While we mindlessly use our technology to push back the darkness, to the pre-electric mind, the days growing shorter really meant shorter days, and longer darkness. We may discover the winter solstice in our calendars or hear about it as a quick item on our news reports, but those who came before us were critically aware that their world was shrinking, that less was now available to them, and so they directed faith towards the point of return. For them, the winter solstice was a turning point—an end and a new beginning. That is why every culture has a mid-winter holiday. That is the origin of the dying and rising river gods of Egypt. That is the true source of the tale of Persephone, the Greek princess who spends six months in the underworld. That is why Druids burned trees and wickermen. Each of these moments is a chance to rage against the darkness, to burn fire into the night to show the light how to return.

Every time we talk about night, fire, darkness, and light, we have meaning. Instantaneously, good and evil, ignorance and knowledge, and other dualities enter the conversation. Illumination does that—it is a kind of symbolic spontaneous combustion. That is why the Hanukkah candles have meaning long before they are understood. Inherently, the very act of lighting up the darkness is a redemptive process. Somehow, in each and all of our tellings of the Hanukkah story, somewhere in the bottom-line meaning or plot, we kindle a light rather than curse the darkness. In that single flame, hope is reborn.

CONCEPTS

LIGHTS

The central mitzvah of Hanukkah is to kindle lights. These lights serve as physical reminders of the miracle of Hanukkah—the triumph of the few over the many, the fight for religious freedom in the face of the threat of forced assimilation. They act as a concrete symbol of the resolve to "publicize" the miracle of Hanukkah, to ourselves and our families, to the neighborhood - indeed, to the world.

Interestingly, the origin of the lights is probably not Jewish at all. Many pagan religions observed winter solstice torch festivals to enlighten the darkest days of the year. As the story is told in the *First Book of Maccabees*, Judah rekindled the menorah of the Temple after cleansing it. Jews adapted the practice of candlelighting to the Hanukkah holiday. And, although the practice was rooted in pagan customs, the religious leadership of the people infused it with religious significance. The rabbis of the Talmud, some 364 years later, recorded the famous legend of the single cruse of oil that miraculously lasted eight days to give a religious meaning to this popular practice. Since then, rabbinic authorities surrounded the ritual of candlelighting with specific laws and customs designed to make this act fully Jewish. (Even the requirement for the candles to be in one line reflects the rabbis' concern that one should not think that the *hanukkiyah* was representative of a torch, the kind of torch used in the ancient pagan rituals.)

How important is it to kindle Hanukkah lights? The rabbis said that if a person must choose between buying supplies for Hanukkah lights and wine for the Shabbat Kiddush, the Hanukkah lights are to be acquired first. Even if one is studying Torah, the lesson must stop in order to kindle the *hanukkiyah*.

WHY EIGHT LIGHTS?

Some scholars believe that the Hanukkah rededication of the Temple celebration was patterned after the original eight-day dedication of Solomon's Temple. A similar eight-day celebration was held for the opening of the Second Temple in the time of Ezra and Nehemiah. Moreover, the rededication of the Temple presented the religious Maccabees with the first opportunity they had to celebrate the most recent major holiday, Sukkot, an eight-day festival.

> "The sanctuary was purified on the twenty-fifth day of Kislev...This joyful celebration went on for eight days; it was like Sukkot, for they recalled how only a short time before they had kept the festival while living like animals in the mountains; and so they carried *lulavim* and *etrogim*, and

they chanted hymns (Hallel) to God who had triumphantly led them to
the purification of His Temple...

II Maccabees 10

Of course, the most popular legend to explain the eight lights is the single jug of oil
that miraculously lasted eight days instead of just one. While this story is well-known, if
we think carefully about it, we realize that the miracle was not that the oil lasted eight
days. After all, we would have expected the oil to last one day. So, shouldn't the miracle
be considered seven days?

No ordinary oil could be used for lighting the Temple menorah. The special, pure
olive oil for this purpose was carefully produced under the supervision of the priests and
their seal was put on each jug. The jug of oil Judah found had this seal upon it. As soon
as the oil began to burn, Judah initiated the process of producing more of this special
oil. It took three days to travel to the area where the best olives grew, and three days to
return to Jerusalem.

Then, one more day was required to press the olives and purify the oil, making a total
of seven days. The miracle is that the single jug of oil burned exactly the amount of time
required for new oil to be manufactured and brought to Jerusalem.

PUBLICIZE THE MIRACLE

According to Maimonides, the famous twelfth-century redactor of Jewish law, the
commandment to light the *hanukkiyah* is exceedingly important.

> One should carefully fulfill it (the obligation to light the Hanukkah
> lights) in order to publicize the miracle and to offer additional praise
> and thanksgiving to God for the wonders which He did for us.
>
> Even if a person has no food to eat, he should beg or sell his garment in
> order to buy oil and lamps and light them.
>
> Maimonides, *Hilkhot Hanukkah 4:12*

Clearly, something very important is happening here. As we shall see, the *hanukkiyah*
itself is to be hung outside the home, on the doorpost opposite the *mezuzah*. Why this
nearly fanatic concern for Jews to *pirsumei nisa*—"publicize" the miracle?

For the rabbis, the very purpose of Hanukkah was to celebrate the victory of religious
belief over the forces of assimilation. The lighting of the *hanukkiyah* is the vehicle by
which we remember this moment of Jewish history and proclaim it to ourselves and the
outside world.

OBJECTS

THE *HANUKKIYAH*

The Hanukkah menorah, called a *hanukkiyah* in Hebrew, is the candelabrum designed to hold the lights (often, but not always, candles) of Hanukkah. It is an adaptation of the ancient menorah of the Holy Temple, one of the earliest symbols of the Jewish people.

Described in detail in the Bible (Exodus 25:31-37), the menorah was probably a physical representation of the Tree of Life of the Garden of Eden. It had seven branches and was often seen as representing the seven days of creation. The menorah was one of the central features of the Temple; its lamps served as a source of light from evening to morning. Its central lamp was never allowed to burn out; this is the source of the *Ner Tamid*—"Eternal Light"—we find to this day in modern synagogues.

The Temple menorah burned pure, beaten olive oil, oil that was produced in olive presses supervised by representatives of the priesthood. The oil was packaged in containers and sealed with the special mark of the High Priest to distinguish it from ordinary oil. This requirement, of course, is an important part of the famous "one jug of oil" legend of Hanukkah.

When Judah the Maccabee decreed an eight-day holiday to commemorate the rededication of the Temple, our ancestors began to kindle the eight lights of the festival. At first, people would simply line up ordinary clay oil lamps. But since multiple lamps of this type were required, the need for a single lamp with multiple wicks became evident.

The major difference between the Temple menorah and the *hanukkiyah* is the number of branches—the menorah of the Temple had seven branches, while the later *hanukkiyah* has nine (lamps—not always branches). The development of the *hanukkiyah* as both a ritual tool and an *objet d'art* is fascinating. Most early *hanukkiyot* burned olive oil and were made from either stone or metal. Since the *hanukkiyah* was originally to be placed outside the entrance of the household, lanterns were probably used to protect the flames from the wind. Similarly, back-walls developed in *hanukkiyot* dating from the 13th century in order to facilitate the hanging of the *hanukkiyah* on a wall or doorpost. The innovation of the back-wall enabled Jewish artisans to develop distinctive motifs for *hanukkiyot*, often revealing artistic influences from surrounding cultures. (See *Encyclopedia Judaica*, Volume 7, pages 1288-1315, for photographs of representative *hanukkiyot*.)

WHY *HANUKKIYOT* HAVE A *SHAMASH*

While eight lights are required on the *ḥanukkiyah*, one to be lit each night of Hanukkah, it became customary for the Hanukkah menorah to have place for *nine* flames. The ninth flame is called the *shamash*—"the servant"—for its purpose is to light the others. The reason for the *shamash* probably derives from the legal principle that the Hanukkah lights themselves are not to be used for any purpose other than to "publicize the miracle." Thus, a "servant flame" is needed to light the other eight, keeping them from serving a pragmatic function (like lighting another flame.)

BASIC *HANUKKIYOT* LAWS

The *ḥanukkiyah* may be made out of any material. Metals, ceramics, even woods are common. Some prefer metal to remember one of the stories given for the eight lights. *Pesikta Rabbati*, an early collection of *midrashim*, records that when the Maccabees entered the Temple, they found eight metal spears left by the Greeks, from which they fashioned the first *ḥanukkiyah*—a kind of prototypic beating of spears into eternal light.

The freedom of expression enjoyed by modern Jewish artisans has resulted in a panoply of beautiful *ḥanukkiyot*. The only caution about their form is that the receptacles for the lights should form a straight row—not a circle or semi-circle, lest the flames appear as a torch. The reason for this is to ensure that one can tell by a glance at the *ḥanukkiyah* which night of Hanukkah is being celebrated. It may also have something to do with the rabbis' attempt to remove any hint of the pagan torch festivals from which the winter solstice candlelighting was originally adapted.

It is customary to acquire the most beautiful *ḥanukkiyah* one can afford in order to fulfill the precept of *hiddur mitzvah*, the embellishment or beautification of a basic commandment. In recent years, Jewish artisans have created spectacular *ḥanukkiyot*, rendering the old green "souvenir of Israel" menorahs quite unfashionable. If you do not already own a *ḥanukkiyah*, or wish to give your family a wonderful Hanukkah gift, purchase one of these modern pieces of Jewish ritual art. It will become an important family heirloom in years to come.

On the other hand, the greatest "beautification" of Hanukkah may be to create your own *ḥanukkiyot*. Certainly, families who use *ḥanukkiyot* made by children in school or by families in workshops fulfill the notion of *hiddur mitzvah* as much or more so than buying an expensive piece of art.

To this day, many families acquire and light *ḥanukkiyot* that utilize oil as fuel. Undoubtedly, the feeling of authenticity of this type of Hanukkah lamp adds much to the flavor of the celebration. Olive oil is preferred for it is drawn easily into the wick, its light is pure and clear in color, and, of course, it reminds us of the actual olive oil used in the Temple. Wicks made of any material are acceptable, although cotton or linen are the wicks of choice. The wicks may be relit each night until used up.

Since olive oil is not readily available in many of the places Jews have found themselves throughout history, wax candles were permitted for use in the *ḥanukkiyah*. Specially-made Hanukkah candles are readily available during the season. Unlike Shabbat candles, Hanukkah candles need not be white. In fact, one of the joys of the holiday is to see the multicolored candles aflame in the *ḥanukkiyah*. Hanukkah candles are also much shorter than Shabbat candles since they are only required to burn for one-half hour.

All candles should be of the same height, although the *shamash* is usually placed higher (although it could be lower) in order to distinguish it from the other eight candles. Most *ḥanukkiyot* allow for this in their design.

PRACTICE

Lighting the *ḥanukkiyah* is the major ritual act of the Hanukkah festival. As such, the procedures for kindling the Hanukkah lights, while not complicated, have been precisely outlined for us.

The first decision to be made is where to place the *ḥanukkiyah(ot)*. If you interpret the dictum "publicize the miracle" to refer to the outside world, you may decide to place the *ḥanukkiyah* in a window sill or even outdoors. This is the preferred practice. If "publicize the miracle" refers to your own family, choose any convenient central location in the home, perhaps on a fireplace mantle, a breakfront, the dining room table, or another location in the major traffic pattern of the house. Many families create a "candlelighting center" for Hanukkah, surrounded by decorations, presents, greeting cards, dreidles, etc.

A cautionary tip: Place sheets of aluminum foil or trays under the *ḥanukkiyah(ot)* in order to catch dripping wax or even to prevent the spread of fire. Don't laugh. A number of years ago, our friends Jerry and Ruby Bubis lit their *ḥanukkiyah* one night before leaving to visit friends and returned to find their entire home had burned down because of a fallen Hanukkah candle. If you must leave the house while the lights are burning, be sure to position the *ḥanukkiyah(ot)* in a safe place.

The *ḥanukkiyah(ot)* should not be moved after the lights are kindled. It can, however, be repositioned from night to night.

Virtually all Jews kindle the lights of the *ḥanukkiyah* beginning with one light on the first night of Hanukkah, two lights on the second night, and so forth until all eight lights of the *ḥanukkiyah* are burning on the eighth and final night of the holiday. What you may not realize is that there was a great debate among the disciples of two of the most famous rabbis of the Talmud concerning this practice. The School of Shammai argued that all eight lights should be kindled on the first night and that on each subsequent night one light should be taken away. The School of Hillel countered that the purpose of the holiday is to "increase our joy," so they began the holiday with one light per night, gradually adding an additional light each night.

Why are there two candlelighting traditions included in the Gemara? There are two answers: the practical and the ideological. The practical reason for two suggestions is that the rabbis probably did not really know how to do the ritual. It had developed among the people and different groups most likely followed different practices. The ideological reason reflects one of the great hallmarks of Judaism—its embrace of pluralism. Although the rabbis had to settle on one practice, they included the discussion and reasoning for both traditions in the official record of their deliberations.

Of course, the practice of the School of Hillel was adopted as the standard ritual and our modern candlelighting ceremony is descended from this decision.

The placement of the candles in the *hanukkiyah* and the proper procedure for kindling the lights is often one of the most misunderstood aspects of the ritual. Actually, it is quite simple if you remember the following guideline:

SET TO THE LEFT.

LIGHT TO THE RIGHT.

The basic pattern of placing the candles is:

1.   Set the *shamash* in its holder.

2.   Place the candle for the first night in the far right holder.

      (This is the set-up for the first night of Hanukkah.)

3.   On the second night, repeat steps 1 and 2 and add a candle in the next holder toward the left of the first night's candle.

4.   On each subsequent night, continue to add one candle toward the left until, on the eighth night, all holders are filled.

The procedure for kindling the lights is:

1.   Light the *shamash*.

2.   Say/Chant the *b'rakhot*.

      On the first night of Hanukkah, three blessings are recited:

      a.   *L'hadlik ner shel Hanukkah.*

b. *Sheh'asah nissim la'avoteinu.*

c. *Shebeheyanu.*

On the second and subsequent nights of Hanukkah, only the first two blessings are recited:

a. *L'hadlik ner shel Hanukkah.*

b. *Sheh'asah nissim la'avoteinu.*

3. Using the *shamash*, **light the newest candle first.**

   (Option: Some begin to kindle the lights while reciting *Sheh'asah nissim.*)

4. When all the lights are kindled, place the *shamash* in its holder.

5. Say/Chant *Ha-neirot Hallalu, Maoz Tzur* and other Hanukkah songs.

First Night

Second Night

Third Night

Fourth Night

Fifth Night

Sixth Night

Seventh Night

Eighth Night

One way to remember the proper procedure is to keep in mind that we kindle the light representing the specific night of Hanukkah first, before lighting the others. Thus, on the fifth night of Hanukkah, we kindle the fifth light first, then the fourth, the third, and so on. Each night's light is given the honor of being lit first.

One of the most difficult tasks of the lighting process, if you use candles, is getting them to stay put in the *hanukkiyah*. A tip: Using a long match or the *shamash*, melt a few drops of wax from the end of each candle into its receptacle in the *hanukkiyah*. Then, firmly place the candle into the bottom of the receptacle and hold for a few seconds. The melted wax will form a seal with the candle to hold it in place. However, when it is time to put the *shamash* in its receptacle, do not use the flame of an already-lit candle to melt its bottom. (Remember: the Hanukkah lights are not to be used for any purpose other than publicizing the miracle.) Use a match to melt the bottom of the *shamash*. Alternatively, some families place aluminum foil in the receptacles to help steady the candles.

The paragraph *Ha-neirot Hallalu* is sung while kindling the lights. It states the reason why we kindle "these lights"—to recall the wondrous triumphs and miraculous victories. We are also reminided that we are not to use the lights for any "ordinary" purpose, but rather we are to look upon them and remember to thank God for the miracle of our deliverance.

According to the Ashkenazic tradition (Jews from East European ancestry), the song *Maoz Tzur* is chanted immediately after the lights are kindled. This most famous of Hanukkah songs was written more than 600 years ago by a poet named Mordecai It also praises God for saving the Jewish people.

The Sephardim (Jews from Spanish and Arabic speaking countries) recite Psalm 30 *"Mizmor Shir Hanukkat ha-Bayit L'David"* after kindling the lights.

PRACTICAL QUESTIONS AND ANSWERS

When are the Hanukkah lights lit?

The Talmud says the proper time for kindling the Hanukkah lights is "from the time the sun sets." Defining what is meant by this time varies according to whom one asks. Some authorities prefer lighting immediately at the beginning of sunset. Others prescribe 13-40 minutes after sunset. Since there is no prohibition against kindling lights on the holiday itself, the exact minute of candlelighting is not especially important. If one is not able to kindle lights after sunset, it is permissible to light before sunset, but only if the lights themselves will last the half hour after sunset. If one forgets to light at the proper time, lights may be kindled any time during the evening.

How long must the Ḥanukkah lights burn?

The legal requirement is that the candles burn "until the time that people cease to walk about in the street" (*Shabbat 21b*). Before the advent of street lighting, people did not usually walk about at night long after nightfall. In fact, it was somewhat dangerous to do so. Since the practice of the people was to be in their homes within one-half hour after nightfall, and the primary mitzvah was "publicizing the miracle of Ḥanukkah," the practice of displaying the Ḥanukkah lights was designed for pedestrian traffic. Therefore, the rabbis decided that the Ḥanukkah lights should last one-half hour after three stars appear.

Where is the *ḥanukkiyah* placed?

The Talmud specifies where the Ḥanukkah menorah is to be located:

> "One should place the Ḥanukkah lamp by the door of the house, on the outside, within a handbreadth of the door, so that it is on the left side of a person entering the house, the *mezuzah* on the right and the Ḥanukkah lamp on the left. If one resides in an upper story, the lamp should be placed in a window overlooking the public domain…In times of danger, one may place the Ḥanukkah lamp inside the house, on the table…"
>
> *Shabbat 21b*

Today, many people place the *ḥanukkiyah* in a window facing the street to comply with the requirement to "publicize the miracle." Other families interpret the need to "publicize the miracle" to refer to one's own family and create a Ḥanukkah candlelighting center somewhere within the home, often on a low counter or table where children can reach the *ḥanukkiyah*.

The practice of some groups to make a public spectacle of candlelighting (often on public and government sites) is derived from this mitzvah "to publicize the miracle." We will deal with the controversy engendered by public candlelightings in Part II.

Who is obligated to light the *ḥanukkiyah*?

The Talmud specifies three options. At the very least, each household is to light a single candle on each of the eight nights. In the home of the "*mehadrin*"—the "zealous"—each member of the family lights one candle every night. The most zealous—"*mehadrin min ha-mehadrin*"—light one candle on the first night and one additional candle is added each subsequent night.

Our practice is that of the most zealous, that is, we add a light each night of the holiday until we reach the required eight. Many families acquire a *ḥanukkiyah* for each person to light, although others light only one *ḥanukkiyah* according to this practice.

Is there any requirement that a woman or a man is to light the *ḥanukkiyah*?

Women and men are equally obligated to kindle Ḥanukkah lights. In fact, men and women who are single or single parents are required to light a *ḥanukkiyah*.

May children light their own *ḥanukkiyot*?

Yes. In fact, if children have made a *ḥanukkiyah* at religious school, encourage them to use it. However, the adult(s) in the family may not transfer their obligation to light a *ḥanukkiyah* for themselves. Some authorities would say that the obligation for children to light the *ḥanukkiyah* begins with their becoming a Bar or Bat Mitzvah.

What if I'm visiting another family? Should I bring our family *ḥanukkiyah* to light?

According to Jewish law, you could join in the lighting and blessings of the *ḥanukkiyah* in someone else's home. But, most families would consider the addition of your Ḥanukkah menorah(s) an enhancement of their celebration.

Can an electric menorah be used as a *ḥanukkiyah*?

According to nearly all authorities, an electrified menorah may not be used to fulfill the mitzvah of kindling the Ḥanukkah lights. While electric bulbs undoubtedly give off light, the filaments are not considered a "flame." Moreover, a requisite amount of "fuel" must be available when the lights are kindled. An electric menorah depends on continuous generation of power to remain lit. Thus, the act of kindling in itself is insufficient to cause the lamp to burn for the prescribed period of time. Since the *halakhic* principle governing the *ḥanukkiyah* is "kindling constitutes the performance of the mitzvah," turning on an electric light would not fulfill the commandment.

Some oil *ḥanukkiyot* have one reservoir for oil and separate wicks. Is this permitted?

Yes, as long as the wicks are separated so they appear as separate lights and not like a torch.

May I read by the light of the *ḥanukkiyah*?

No. Unlike the Shabbat candles, the Ḥanukkah lights are not to be used for any purpose other than to publicize the miracle of Ḥanukkah. So, do not eat your Ḥanukkah dinner by the candlelight of the *ḥanukkiyah*. If you would enjoy a candlelit home, light separate tapers in addition to the *ḥanukkiyah*.

Is it true that I should not do any work while the Ḥanukkah lights are burning?

Yes. Our attention should be focused on the lights during the half-hour that they burn.

May I light one Hanukkah candle with another?

No, not with a candle meant to be representative of one of the nights of Hanukkah. This is the reason for the *shamash*—the servant candle. It is lit first and used to light all the others.

If we are lighting more than one *hanukkiyah*, does each one have to have a *shamash*?

Yes. In order to ensure that the Hanukkah candles are not used for lighting each other, each *hanukkiyah* should have a *shamash*.

What do I do if the *shamash* goes out?

Relight it, but not from the flame of one of the Hanukkah candles. Use a match.

What do I do if one of the Hanukkah lights goes out?

Since the primary mitzvah is the lighting itself, if a light should go out after the blessings are said, it is not necessary to rekindle the light.

May I blow the candles out?

No. The lights are to be left alone to burn out. Each night, new candles should be used. If, however, there is more oil than needed for the minimum half-hour of burning, you may extinguish the wicks in an oil-burning *hanukkiyah* after the required half-hour and relight them the next evening.

May longer candles than the standard Hanukkah candles be used?

Yes. The candles are to last a *minimum* of one half-hour.

How many candles will we light during Hanukkah?

Forty-four, the exact number that happen to come in most packages of Hanukkah candles.

Do the colors of the candles have any significance at all?

No. They just add to the joy of the holiday. Actually, a number of people we spoke to recall as children trying to vary the colors as they set up their *hanukkiyot*, creating a rainbow effect that is quite beautiful.

Why is the *Shebeheyanu* recited only on the first night of Hanukkah while the *Sheh'asah nissim* is said each night of the festival?

The *Shebeheyanu* prayer thanks God for enabling us to reach this special time, and thus is said only on the first night. The *Sheh'asah nissim* is said every night because a "miracle" occurred each day of the holiday.

When Shabbat candles are lit, the custom is to block one's view of the lights while saying the blessings. Why don't we do the same when lighting the *hanukkiyah*?

The usual practice of Jewish ritual is to say the blessing first, followed by the act itself. For example, we recite the *Ha-Motzi* and then eat bread. Recall that on Shabbat, once we say the blessing, it is Shabbat and we cannot light a fire. That is why the rabbis developed the strategy of preparing the lights before saying the blessing on Shabbat. But, on Hanukkah, this is unnecessary and thus, we say the blessings and then kindle the lights.

Speaking of Shabbat, when are the Hanukkah lights lit on Friday evening?

With the prohibition against lighting fire on Shabbat, Hanukkah lights are kindled immediately *before* the Shabbat candles on Friday evening. So, the procedure would be to first, set up the Hanukkah candles, recite the Hanukkah blessings, and then light the Hanukkah candles. Next, kindle the Shabbat candles and recite the blessing for the Shabbat lights. Since we light Shabbat candles at least 18 minutes before sunset, some use extra long candles for the *hanukkiyah* on Shabbat Hanukkah so that they last at least thirty minutes after sunset.

What about lighting the *hanukkiyah* on Saturday night? Which comes first, Hanukkah lights or Havdalah?

Most rabbinic authorities hold that Hanukkah lights are lit *after* Havdalah. This guards against the possibility of violating the Shabbat by lighting a fire. Havdalah marks the separation between the sacred time of the Sabbath and the "ordinary" time of the work week, physically demonstrated by the lighting of the Havdalah candle. Hanukkah candles are lit immediately after the conclusion of the Havdalah service. In the synagogue the Hanukkah lights are lit before the recitation of Havdalah.

Are there any other adaptations of home rituals during the Hanukkah celebration?

Yes. During the *Birkat ha-Mazon*, the prayer *Al ha-Nissim* is added before the section *V'al ha-Kol*. Also, since *Rosh Hodesh Tevet* (the first of the Hebrew month of *Tevet*) always occurs during Hanukkah, we add the paragraph for *Rosh Hodesh* in *Birkat ha-Mazon* as well on those days. (See *The Art of Jewish Living: The Shabbat Seder* for the complete *Birkat ha-Mazon*, including the placement of *Al ha-Nissim*.) *Al ha-Nissim* is also added to the *Amidah* in the daily prayers.

Must I light the *hanukkiyah* if I see it lit in the synagogue?

It is true that most synagogues light a *hanukkiyah* during the eight days of the holiday. However, this does not release one from lighting at home.

HADLAKAT NEIROT—
CANDLELIGHTING

1. Barukh atah Adonai	1 Praised are You, Adonai,
2. Eloheinu melekh ha-olam	2. Our God, Ruler of the universe,
3. Asher kidshanu	3 who made us holy
4. b'mitzvotav	4. through the commandments
5. V'tzivanu	5. and commanded us
6. L'hadlik ner shel Hanukkah.	6. to kindle the Hanukkah lights.
7. Barukh atah Adonai	7. Praised are You, Adonai,
8. Eloheinu melekh ha-olam,	8. Our God, Ruler of the universe,
9. Sheh'asah nissim	9. who performed wondrous deeds
10. la'avoteinu	10. for our ancestors
11. Ba-yamim ha-heim	11. in those (ancient) days
12. Ba-z'man ha-zeh	12. at this season.

(on the first night only):

13. Barukh atah Adonai	13. Praised are You, Adonai,
14. Eloheinu melekh ha-olam	14. Our God, Ruler of the universe,
15. shehebeyanu	15. Who has given us life
16. v'ki-y'manu	16. and sustained us
17. v'higiyanu	17. and enabled us to reach
18. la-z'man ha-zeh.	18. this season.

1. בָּרוּךְ אַתָּה יהוה
2. אֱלֹהֵינוּ מֶלֶךְ הָעוֹלָם
3. אֲשֶׁר קִדְּשָׁנוּ
4. בְּמִצְוֹתָיו
5. וְצִוָּנוּ
6. לְהַדְלִיק נֵר שֶׁל חֲנֻכָּה.

7. בָּרוּךְ אַתָּה יהוה
8. אֱלֹהֵינוּ מֶלֶךְ הָעוֹלָם
9. שֶׁעָשָׂה נִסִּים
10. לַאֲבוֹתֵינוּ
11. בַּיָּמִים הָהֵם
12. בַּזְּמַן הַזֶּה.

13. בָּרוּךְ אַתָּה יהוה
14. אֱלֹהֵינוּ מֶלֶךְ הָעוֹלָם
15. שֶׁהֶחֱיָנוּ
16. וְקִיְּמָנוּ
17. וְהִגִּיעָנוּ
18. לַזְּמַן הַזֶּה.

5

הַנֵּרוֹת הַלָּלוּ

HA-NEIROT HALLALU

Hanukkah was a very exciting holiday. I did not get to light a candle each night because we had more children than there were candles, but there was always a race to see which candles would last the longest.

Rae Gindi

Let's study a Jewish prayer. It is called *Ha-neirot Hallalu* and it is the short paragraph which is now said (by force of tradition) after the three *b'rakhot* (two after the first night), while the *hanukkiyah* is burning. It is of early Gaonic origin, which means that it was created by rabbinic scholars who lived shortly after the redaction of the Talmud, probably around 700 C.E.

> These lights we kindle (to recall)
> the miracles and the wonders and the deliverance and the victories
> (battles)
> that our ancestors accomplished
> in those days at this season through the hands of Your holy priests.
> And throughout all eight days of Hanukkah
> these lights are sanctified and we may not use them
> except to look upon them in order to thank and praise Your great name
> for Your miracle and for Your wonders and for Your deliverance.

This short prayer is as close as the tradition comes to presenting an authorized explanation of Hanukkah. Its origins are in a Talmudic-like but post-Talmudic work called *Masekhet Sofrim*. There, in chapter 20, a series of Hanukkah rules are presented, along with some instructions for observing *Rosh Hodesh*, the New Month. The connection between these two Jewish celebrations is that Hallel, a series of psalms of praise, is added to the morning liturgy on both occasions—and Hanukkah always includes *Rosh Hodesh Tevet*.

1

What's interesting about the account in *Sofrim* is what has been added, and what has been changed. Let's look at it closely.

> These lights we kindle (to recall)
> the **miracles** and the **wonders** and the **deliverance** and the **victories**
> (battles)...

This time, Hanukkah is described, not only as the celebration of a miracle (the little jug of oil that could), but in the same terms as the Exodus, "miracles and wonders." Look at the similarity to this verse, Deuteronomy 26:8:

Then the Lord took us out of Egypt with a mighty hand, with an out-stretched arm, with **awesome power,** with **signs**, and with **wonders.**

And to these three verses at the end of the Torah:

Never again will Israel have a prophet like Moses who knew the Lord face to face. Who did all the **signs** and **wonders** which God sent him to do in the land of Egypt; to Pharaoh and all his workers, and all his land. And all the mighty hand, and all the **wonders** which Moses made happen before the eyes of all Israel.

What was implied in the earliest Hanukkah texts, and what was hidden in the Talmudic accounts, is suddenly made clear here through the use of literary allusion. The victory of the Maccabees was as much a sign of God's involvement in history, as much an act of Redemption, as was the premier, archetypical first salvation of Israel, the Exodus from Egypt. By appropriating the language of the Exodus to talk about Hanukkah, the Gaonic authors of this prayer establish the connection and make that spiritual statement. Compare it to the Talmudic rabbis' formulation in the second *b'rakhah*.:

Praised are You, Adonai, Our God, Ruler of the universe, who performed miracles for our ancestors in those (ancient) days at this season.

In the original (probably Talmudic) formulation, Hanukkah is about some sort of "miracles" (unspecified) with the focus being our familiar passage from *Shabbat 21b*, the story of the jug of oil:

For when the Greeks entered the Temple, they defiled all of the oil in it, and when the Hasmonean dynasty defeated them, they searched and found only one jug of oil with the official seal of the Head *Kohein*, enough to burn for one day. But a miracle happened and the oil lasted for eight days.

2

that our ancestors accomplished
in those days at this season through the hands of Your holy priests...

When we compare *Ha-neirot Hallalu* to the Talmudic version, the differing description of the "Maccabees" and their role(s) is significant. In the Talmud, the Hasmonean dynasty, a secular political force, enters the Temple. In *Ha-neirot Hallalu*, priestly leaders, the Hashmon family, lead the people to a military victory with God's help. In the Talmud, the victory was totally a human accomplishment. Here, the Maccabees have again become God's true agents.

3

And throughout all eight days of Hanukkah
these lights are sanctified and we may not use them...

Here in the midst of telling a story, *Ha-neirot Hallalu* reteaches us a *halakhah*, a Jewish rule. It is a direct echo of a Talmudic passage, as well:

> One cannot use the Hanukkah lamp for personal needs, for that one must have an additional lamp. If, however, one has kindled a torch as a Hanukkah lamp, no additional lamp is required.
>
> *Ibid.*

But, as we will see in the last portion of this prayer, this law about practice can reveal an important message.

4

except to look upon them in order to thank and praise Your great name
for Your miracles and for Your wonders and for Your deliverance...

Now, we understand that the Hanukkah lights may only serve one purpose, human
inspiration. Their job is to enlighten us. When we gaze into the flames transfixed, we are
to see the power and the majesty of God. But it is more than that. The prayer contains a
wonderful contradiction in its repetition, a contradiction whose resolution is a wonderful Hanukkah lesson:

On the one hand, God is credited with the Hanukkah miracles. In contradistinction,
the first part of the prayer credits our ancestors:

> the miracles and the wonders and the deliverance and the victories
> (battles)
> that our ancestors accomplished...

The contradiction is of course easily resolved. God works through people. Some human
accomplishments are Divine miracles.

The lesson of *Ha-neirot Hallalu* is powerful. Hanukkah teaches us how God works.
When people rise up to actualize their potential, God is there. When freedom is won,
God is present. When a dedication or a rededication is made with true religious expression, God is manifest. The candles bring us back to the light the Maccabees rekindled. In
the process, the lights we kindle illuminate our sense of what people can become, and
through that memory, a spiritual awareness of all that God does for us—starting with
who we are.

HA-NEIROT HALLALU
THESE LIGHTS

1. *Ha-neirot hallalu*	1. These lights
2. *Anahnu madlikin*	2. we kindle
3. *Al ha-nissim*	3. (to recall) the miracles
4. *V'al ha-nifla-ot*	4. and the wonders
5. *V'al ha-t'shu-ot*	5. and the deliverance
6. *V'al ha-mil'ha-mot*	6. and the victories (battles)
7. *She'asita la-avoteinu*	7. that our ancestors accomplished
8. *Ba-yamim ha-heim*	8. in those days
9. *Ba-z'man ha-zeh*	9. at this season
10. *Al y'dei kohanekha ha-k'doshim.*	10. through the hands of Your holy priests.
11. *V'khol sh'monat y'mei Hanukkah*	11. And throughout all eight days of Hanukkah
12. *Ha-neirot hallalu kodesh heim,*	12. these lights are sanctified
13. *V'ein lanu r'shut*	13. and we may not
14. *L'hishtameish ba-hem*	14. use them
15. *Elah lirotam bilvad,*	15. except to look upon them
16. *K'dei l'hodot u-le'haleil*	16. in order to thank and praise
17. *L'shimkha ha-gadol*	17. Your great name
18. *Al nisekha v'al nifl'otekha*	18. for Your miracles and for Your wonders
19. *V'al y'shu-ah-tekhah.*	19. and for Your deliverance.

1. הַנֵּרוֹת הַלָּלוּ
2. אֲנַחְנוּ מַדְלִיקִין
3. עַל הַנִּסִּים
4. וְעַל הַנִּפְלָאוֹת
5. וְעַל הַתְּשׁוּעוֹת
6. וְעַל הַמִּלְחָמוֹת
7. שֶׁעָשִׂיתָ לַאֲבוֹתֵינוּ
8. בַּיָּמִים הָהֵם
9. בַּזְּמַן הַזֶּה
10. עַל יְדֵי כֹּהֲנֶיךָ הַקְּדוֹשִׁים.
11. וְכָל־שְׁמוֹנַת יְמֵי חֲנֻכָּה
12. הַנֵּרוֹת הַלָּלוּ קֹדֶשׁ הֵם
13. וְאֵין לָנוּ רְשׁוּת
14. לְהִשְׁתַּמֵּשׁ בָּהֶם
15. אֶלָּא לִרְאוֹתָם בִּלְבָד,
16. כְּדֵי לְהוֹדוֹת וּלְהַלֵּל
17. לְשִׁמְךָ הַגָּדוֹל
18. עַל נִסֶּיךָ וְעַל נִפְלְאוֹתֶיךָ
19. וְעַל יְשׁוּעָתֶךָ.

6

מָעוֹז צוּר
MAOZ TZUR

The purpose of this meditation on *Maoz Zur* is to reclaim it for the liturgical enrichment of Ḥanukkah. The sudden popularity of Ḥanukkah, spurred by Zionist achievement and American need, has outgrown the traditional liturgical garb, predicated on a different valence for the festival. In this bind, we are ill-served by dispensing with a poetic ornament that actually accords with our historical and religious sensibilities. Nor should we be satisfied with an act of tokenism—the retention of a single stanza mistranslated to mask its real meaning.

Ismar Schorsch

MAOZ TZUR

Maoz Tzur is undoubtedly the most famous of Hanukkah songs. Composed in the thirteenth century of the Common Era by a poet only known to us through the acrostic found in the first letters of the original five stanzas of the song - Mordecai - it became the traditional hymn sung after the candlelighting in Ashkenazi homes. The familiar tune is most probably a derivation of a German Protestant church hymn or a popular folk song.

Although many families attempt to sing the first stanza, either in the original Hebrew or in a not-so-accurate English translation by M. Jastrow and G. Gottheil entitled "Rock of Ages," the song as it has evolved through the years now contains six stanzas, the last stanza having been added by an unknown poet sometime during the sixteenth century. Unfortunately, due either to the exuberance of children rushing to open presents or the general illiteracy with regard to Jewish liturgy, *Maoz Tzur* often gets a token singing at best, with the vast majority of Hanukkah celebrants quite unaware of its true meaning.

In a fascinating look at *Maoz Tzur*, Professor Ismar Schorsch, Chancellor of the Jewish Theological Seminary of America, examined the text of the poem in a penetrating article entitled "A Meditation on *Maoz Zur*" (*Judaism*, Fall, 1988, pp. 459-464) Explaining that he and his family fled from Germany on the first day of Hanukkah, 1938, Schorsch says the singing of *Maoz Tzur* has always held special significance for him. Yet, he wonders, why was it that their practice was to sing the first five stanzas and not the later sixth?

The theme of *Maoz Tzur* is a familiar one: God's unfailing redemption of the people Israel. After an opening stanza promising thanksgiving to God now and always, the poet recalls four moments of Divine intervention in chronological order: Egypt, Babylonia, Persia, and the Greeks of the Hanukkah story.

It is the sixth stanza that brings Schorsch to his analysis of the meaning of the poem. In a particularly blunt plea for revenge against the "wicked kingdom," the poet dares to wish for God to intervene once more and "vanquish Christianity in the very shadow of the cross." How could a Jewish poet who knew of the persecutions inflicted on his people by the Romans and their descendants be ignored at the triumphant moment of Hanukkah? Yet, the addition of the sixth stanza calls into question the basic theology of the entire song. If God always redeems his people, why are we still awaiting the messianic kingdom?

Schorsch turns our attention to Psalm 31, upon which the opening phrase "*Maoz Tzur*" is based. The second verse of the Psalm reads: "I seek refuge in You, O Lord; may I never be disappointed; as You are righteous, rescue me." The midrash, the rabbinic commentary that seeks to expound the simple meaning of the text, pounces on the word *"le-olam"*—"never"—and poses one of the most difficult problems for a religious person: how to reconcile the continuous promise of redemption with the harsh reality of life.

In the midrashic dialogue between the people Israel and God, Israel asks why, if God's redemption is everlasting, do we continue to suffer? "To be sure, You have already redeemed us through Moses, through Joshua, and through some judges and kings. But we have once again been subjugated and endure degradation as if we had never been redeemed." God responds that redemption effected through mere mortals is not true redemption, even if influenced by Divine intention.

The author of the sixth stanza of *Maoz Tzur*, reeling from the shock of persecutions and expul-

sions, attached his messianic codicil. The previous redemptions, from the Babylonian exile to the Syrian-Greek oppressions, were of limited duration because they were mediated by men. The fourth kingdom of Christianity will only be overcome by God—directly.

Schorsch concludes that "taken together, the two strata of *Maoz Zur* blend into a liturgical reflection on Jewish history—the precariousness of minority existence, the reality of Divine concern, the consolation of collective memory, and the rarity of true messianism." He warns us to be careful of emphasizing the human role of the Hanukkah story and draws a parallel to the current political situation in Israel. Just as the Maccabees achieved only a limited "redemption," Schorsch warns that "messianism, properly understood, leads to political restraint." The true meaning of *Maoz Tzur* serves both to remind us of the harsh divergence between history and theology and to hold out the promise of ultimate redemption by the hand of God.

MAOZ TZUR—
O MIGHTY ROCK OF MY SALVATION

1. *Maoz tzur y'shu-ah-ti,*

1. O mighty Rock of my salvation,

2. *L'kha na-eh l'shabei-ah.*

2. to praise You is a delight.

3. *Tikkon beit t'filati*

3. Restore my House of Prayer

4. *V'sham*

4. and there

5. *todah n'zabei-ah.*

5. we will bring a thanksgiving offering.

6. *L'eit takhin mat'bei-ah*

6. When You will have prepared the slaughter

7. *Mi-tzar ha-m'nabei'ah,*

7. for the blaspheming foe,

8. *Az egmor b'shir mizmor*

8. Then I shall complete with a song of hymn

9. *Hanukkat ha-miz'bei-ah.*

9. the dedication of the altar.

10. *Ra-ot sav'ah nafshi,*

10. Troubles sated my soul,

11. *B'ya-gon kohi ki-lah.*

11. when with grief my strength was consumed.

12. *Ha-yai meir'ru b'koshi,*

12. They had embittered my life with hardship,

13. *B'shibud malkhut eglah.*

13. with the calf-like kingdom's slavery.

14. *U-v'yado ha-g'dolah*

14. But with His great power

15. *Hotzi et ha-s'gulah,*

15. he brought forth the treasured ones,

16. *Hail Paro v'khol zaro*

16. Pharaoh's army and all his offspring

17. *Yardu k'even bim'tzulah.*

17. went down like a stone into the deep.

1. מָעוֹז צוּר יְשׁוּעָתִי

2. לְךָ נָאֶה לְשַׁבֵּחַ.

3. תִּכּוֹן בֵּית תְּפִלָּתִי

4. וְשָׁם

5. תּוֹדָה נְזַבֵּחַ.

6. לְעֵת תָּכִין מַטְבֵּחַ

7. מִצָּר הַמְנַבֵּחַ.

8. אָז אֶגְמוֹר בְּשִׁיר מִזְמוֹר

9. חֲנֻכַּת הַמִּזְבֵּחַ.

10. רָעוֹת שָׂבְעָה נַפְשִׁי

11. בְּיָגוֹן כֹּחִי כִּלָּה

12. חַיַּי מֵרְרוּ בְקֹשִׁי

13. בְּשִׁעְבּוּד מַלְכוּת עֶגְלָה.

14. וּבְיָדוֹ הַגְּדוֹלָה

15. הוֹצִיא אֶת הַסְּגֻלָּה,

16. חֵיל פַּרְעֹה וְכָל זַרְעוֹ

17. יָרְדוּ כְאֶבֶן בִּמְצוּלָה.

18. D'vir kod'sho hevi'ani.	18. To the abode of His holiness He brought me.
19. V'gam sham lo sha-kat-ti	19. But there, too, I had no rest
20. U'va nogeis v'hig-la-ni.	20. And an oppressor came and exiled me.
21. Ki zarim avad-ti,	21. For I had served aliens,
22. V'yain ra-al masakh-ti.	22. And had drunk benumbing wine.
23. Kim'at she'avar-ti	23. Scarcely had I departed (my land)
24. Keitz bavel,	24. When at Babylonia's demise
Zerubavel—	Zerubabel came—
25. L'keitz shiv'im nosha-ti.	25. At the end of seventy years I was saved.
26. K'rot komat b'rosh	26. To sever the towering cypress*
27. Bikeish Agagi ben Ham-m'data,	27. sought the Aggagite, son of Hammedatha,**
28. V'ni-y'tah lo	28. But it became to him
29. l'fah u-l'mokeish	29. a snare and a stumbling block
30. V'ga-a-va-to nish'batah.	30. and his arrogance was stilled.
31. Rosh y'mini ni-seitah	31. The head of the Benjamite You lifted
32. V'o-yeiv shmo ma-hitah;	32. and the enemy, his name You blotted out;
33. Rov banav v'kin-yanav	33. His numerous progeny—his possessions -
34. Al ha-eitz talitah.	34. on the gallows You hanged.

18. דְּבִיר קָדְשׁוֹ הֱבִיאַנִי

19. וְגַם שָׁם לֹא שָׁקַטְתִּי

20. וּבָא נוֹגֵשׂ וְהִגְלַנִי

21. כִּי זָרִים עָבַדְתִּי

22. וְיֵין רַעַל מָסַכְתִּי

23. כִּמְעַט שֶׁעָבַרְתִּי

24. קֵץ בָּבֶל
זְרֻבָּבֶל

25. לְקֵץ שִׁבְעִים נוֹשַׁעְתִּי.

26. כְּרוֹת קוֹמַת בְּרוֹשׁ

27. בִּקֵּשׁ אֲגָגִי בֶּן הַמְּדָתָא

28. וְנִהְיְתָה לוֹ

29. לְפַח וּלְמוֹקֵשׁ

30. וְגַאֲוָתוֹ נִשְׁבָּתָה.

31. רֹאשׁ יְמִינִי נִשֵּׂאתָ

32. וְאוֹיֵב שְׁמוֹ מָחִיתָ;

33. רֹב בָּנָיו וְקִנְיָנָיו

34. עַל הָעֵץ תָּלִיתָ.

35. *Y'vanim nik-b'tzu alai*
36. *Azai bimei Hash'manim.*
37. *U-fartzu homot mig'dalai*
38. *V-tim'u kol hash'manim;*
39. *U-minotar kankanim*
40. *Na-asah nes la-shoshanim.*
41. *B'nei vinah y'mei shmonah*
42. *Kav'u shir u-r'nanim.*

43. *Ha-sof z'roah kod'shekha*
44. *V'kareiv keitz ha-y'shu-ah—*
45. *N'kom nikmat*
46. *dam avadekha*
47. *Mei-umah ha-r'sha-ah.*
48. *Ki ar'kha lanu ha-y'shuah,*

49. *V'ein keitz li'mei ha-ra'ah,*
50. *D'hei Admon*
51. *b'tzeil tzalmon*
52. *Ha-keim lanu*
53. *ro'im shiv'ah.*

35. Greeks gathered against me
36. then in Hasmonean days.
37. They breached the walls of my towers
38. and they defiled all the oils;
39. And from the one remnant of the flasks
40. a miracle was wrought for the roses.
41. Men of insight—eight days
42. established for song and jubilation.

43. Bare Your holy arm
44. and hasten the End for salvation—
45. Avenge the vengeance
46. of Your servant's blood
47. from the wicked nation.
48. For the triumph is
      too long delayed for us,

49. and there is no end to days of evil.
50. Repel Admon
51. in the shadow of the cross***
52. and establish for us
53. the seven shepherds.****

* Mordecai
** Haman
*** Admon is a derivative of Edom (the Red One), descendants of Esau. This refers to Christianity, perhaps the Papacy.
**** The seven shepherds referred to in Micah 5:4 who will defeat the enemies of Israel are David, Adam, Seth, Methusaleh, Abraham, Jacob, and Moses (see *Sukkah* 52b).

35. יְוָנִים נִקְבְּצוּ עָלַי

36. אֲזַי בִּימֵי חַשְׁמַנִּים.

37. וּפָרְצוּ חוֹמוֹת מִגְדָּלַי

38. וְטִמְּאוּ כָּל הַשְּׁמָנִים;

39. וּמִנּוֹתַר קַנְקַנִּים

40. נַעֲשָׂה נֵס לַשּׁוֹשַׁנִּים.

41. בְּנֵי בִינָה יְמֵי שְׁמוֹנָה

42. קָבְעוּ שִׁיר וּרְנָנִים.

43. חֲשׂוֹף זְרוֹעַ קָדְשֶׁךָ

44. וְקָרֵב קֵץ הַיְשׁוּעָה

45. נְקֹם נִקְמַת

46. דַּם עֲבָדֶיךָ

47. מֵאֻמָּה הָרְשָׁעָה

48. כִּי אָרְכָה לָנוּ הַיְשׁוּעָה.

49. וְאֵין קֵץ לִימֵי הָרָעָה,

50. דְּחֵה אַדְמוֹן

51. בְּצֵל צַלְמוֹן

52. הָקֵם לָנוּ

53. רוֹעִים שִׁבְעָה

A more poetic translation, often sung in English during the candlelighting ceremony, follows:

> Rock of ages, let our song
>
> Praise Your saving power;
>
> You amidst the raging throng
>
> Were our sheltering tower.
>
> Furious they assailed us,
>
> But Your help availed us;
>
> And Your word broke their sword
>
> When our own strength failed us.
>
>
> Children of the martyr race,
>
> Whether free or fettered,
>
> Praise the Lord for all His grace,
>
> Where you may be scattered.
>
> Yours the message cheering
>
> That the time is nearing
>
> Which will see all people free,
>
> Tyrants disappearing.

M. Jastrow and G. Gottheil

7

עַל הַנִּסִּים
AL HA-NISSIM

Nes Gadol Hayah Sham

"A Great Miracle Happened There"

Ḥanukkah Saying

If it is a real Jewish event, it involves food. Everything Jewish involves eating. This is not a secular comment. It is not a joke about the role of the caterer in post-modern Jewish civilization. It has nothing to do with "bagels and lox" Judaism. It was not invented in the Catskills or the Poconos—this is an old Jewish spiritual truth learned in the Torah.

All Jewish prayer starts with eating. Without food, we could not utter a single word of blessing. There is only one place in the Torah where Jews are ordered to bless God. Every single *b'rakhah* Jews say (and that is supposed to be 100 a day) derives from a single biblical verse. In Deuteronomy chapter 8, verse 10 we are told:

> After you have eaten, and you are satisfied,
> you shall bless the Lord your God.

From this verse comes the mitzvah of *Birkat ha-Mazon*, the series of three *b'rakhot* said after eating. From this verse also comes a generalized Talmudic understanding:

> Rav Judah: Samuel taught, To enjoy anything of this world without a *b'rakhah* is like making personal use of things consecrated to heaven...

> Rabbi Hanina ben Papa: To enjoy *anything* in this world without a *b'rakhah* is like robbing the Holy-One-Who-Is-To-Be-Praised and the community of Israel...

> *B'rakhot 35a/b*

It is from this kind of analysis of Deuteronomy 8:10 that the rabbis came to write *b'rakhot* for all kinds of foods, smells, sights, and experiences. Even the daily prayers, the straight *b'rakhot* of praise, grow from this single verse.

Therefore, it is no wonder that *Birkat ha-Mazon* serves a central role in Jewish life. It has a place in every life-cycle event. It grows and becomes special with each holiday. Jews have a notion of a *seudat mitzvah*, a meal in celebration of the performance of *mitzvot*, like weddings and holidays. It is the presence of *Birkat ha-Mazon* which connects the meal to the celebration.

Birkat ha-Mazon changes itself, becoming a customized expression for each occasion. On Purim and Hanukkah (and some add Israel's Independence Day), holidays linked by parallel acts of salvation, an entire paragraph, *Al ha-Nissim*, becomes part of our connection to God at that meal.

The last words of the paragraph before the appearance of *Al ha-Nissim* in the *Birkat ha-Mazon* suggest the appropriateness of adding special words about a particular time of the Jewish year:

> We thank you...for the food we have eaten, for the nourishment You
> provide us all of our days, whatever the season, whatever the time.

At the time of Ḥanukkah, the *Al ha-Nissim* thanks God for "the miracles, the triumphs, the heroism, and the redemption of His people...in the days of Mattathias...and in the days of his sons" when the "evil kingdom of the Greeks rose against Israel, demanding that they abandon Your Torah and violate Your *mitzvot*." The prayer proclaims God's deliverance of "the strong into the hands of the weak, the many into the hands of the few, the corrupt into the hands of the pure in heart, the guilty into the hands of the innocent, and the arrogant into the hands of those who were faithful to Your Torah." Interestingly, and we have seen this often in Jewish liturgy, the prayer is not just a recitation of God's past redemption, but offers hope to the modern reader: "You have wrought great victories and miraculous deliverance for Your people Israel to this day..." The paragraph ends by reminding us that the Hasmonean heroes "set aside these eight days as a season for giving thanks and reciting praises to You," a reference to the saying of the Hallel during Ḥanukkah services.

In short, just as *Ha-neirot Hallalu* offers us a brief history lesson in the reasons for Ḥanukkah as we light the candles each night, the inclusion of *Al ha-Nissim*, both in the *Birkat ha-Mazon* and in the *Amidah* (a central prayer of the three daily prayer services), serve to remind us of the Ḥanukkah story and our obligation to offer thanks to God, our Redeemer.

AL HA-NISSIM
FOR THE MIRACLES

1. *Al ha-nissim*	1.(We thank You) For the miracles
2. *V'al ha-purkan*	2. and for the triumphs
3. *V'al ha-g'vurot*	3. and for the heroism
4. *V'al ha-t'shu-ot*	4. and for the deliverance
5. *V'al ha-mil'ha-mot*	5. and for the battles
6. *Sheh'asita la-avoteinu*	6. that you waged for our ancestors
7. *Ba-yamim ha-heim*	7. in those days
8. *U'va-z'man ha-zeh.*	8. and in our time.
9. *Bimei Matityahu ben Yohanan*	9. In the days of Mattathias son of Yohanan,
10. *Kohein gadol*	10. the High Priest,
11. *Hashmonei u-vanav,*	11. the Hasmonean and his sons,
12. *K'she-amdah malkhut*	12. arose the kingdom
13. *Yavan har'sha-ah*	13. of the evil Greeks
14. *Al amkhah Yisrael*	14. against the people Israel
15. *L'has-ki-ham toratekhah*	15. (demanding) they abandon Your Torah
16. *U-l'ha-aviram*	16. and violate
mei-hu-kei r'tzonekhah.	Your laws;
17. *V'atah b'ra-ha-me-kha ha-rabim*	17. And You in Your great mercy
18. *A'mad'tah la-hem*	18. stood by them
19. *B'eit tza-ra-tam,*	19. in their time of trouble.
20. *Rav'tah et-rivam,*	20. You vindicated them,

1. עַל הַנִּסִּים
2. וְעַל הַפֻּרְקָן
3. וְעַל הַגְּבוּרוֹת
4. וְעַל הַתְּשׁוּעוֹת
5. וְעַל הַמִּלְחָמוֹת
6. שֶׁעָשִׂיתָ לַאֲבוֹתֵינוּ
7. בַּיָּמִים הָהֵם
8. וּבַזְּמַן הַזֶּה.
9. בִּימֵי מַתִּתְיָהוּ בֶּן־יוֹחָנָן
10. כֹּהֵן גָּדוֹל
11. חַשְׁמוֹנַי וּבָנָיו
12. כְּשֶׁעָמְדָה מַלְכוּת
13. יָוָן הָרְשָׁעָה
14. עַל עַמְּךָ יִשְׂרָאֵל
15. לְהַשְׁכִּיחָם תּוֹרָתֶךָ
16. וּלְהַעֲבִירָם
    מֵחֻקֵּי רְצוֹנֶךָ.
17. וְאַתָּה בְּרַחֲמֶיךָ הָרַבִּים
18. עָמַדְתָּ לָהֶם
19. בְּעֵת צָרָתָם,
20. רַבְתָּ אֶת־רִיבָם,

21. *Dan'ta et-dinam,*	21. You defended them,
22. *Na-kam'ta et nik'ma-tam,*	22. You avenged their wrongs.
23. *Masar'ta giborim*	23. You delivered the strong
24. *B'yad ha-lashim,*	24. into the hand of the weak;
25. *V'rabim b'yad m'atim,*	25. and the many into the hand of the few;
26. *U-t'mei-im b'yad t'horim,*	26. and the corrupt into the hand of the pure;
27. *U-r'sha-im b'yad tzadikim,*	27. and the guilty into the hand of the innocent;
28. *V'zeidim b'yad os'kei toratekha.*	28. and the arrogant into the hand of those faithful to your Torah;
29. *U-l'kha asita sheim gadol*	29. And You achieved a great name
30. *V'kadosh b'olamekha,*	30. and Your holiness (is revealed) to the world;
31. *U-l'amkha Yisrael*	31. and for Your people Israel
32. *Asita t'shu-a g'dolah*	32. You wrought a great deliverance
33. *U-furkan k'ha-yom ha-zeh.*	33. and a triumph to this day.
34. *V'ahar kein ba-u va-nekhah*	34. And after this Your children came
35. *Lid'vir bei-tekhah,*	35. to Your Holy of Holies, Your Temple,
36. *U-finu et-hei-kha-lekhah*	36. and to cleanse Your Sanctuary
37. *V'ti-ha-ru et-mik-da-she-khah,*	37. and to purify Your Holy altar
38. *V'hid-li-ku neirot*	38. and to kindle lights
39. *B'hatzrot kod-she-khah,*	39. in Your sacred courts.
40. *V'kav-u sh'monat y'mei Hanukkah ei-lu,*	40. And they set aside these eight days of Hanukkah
41. *L'hodot u-l'hallel*	41. to give thanks and to praise
42. *L'shim-khah ha-gadol.*	42. Your great name.

21.   דַּנְתָּ אֶת־דִּינָם,

22.   נָקַמְתָּ אֶת־נִקְמָתָם,

23.   מָסַרְתָּ גִבּוֹרִים

24.   בְּיַד חַלָּשִׁים,

25.   וְרַבִּים בְּיַד מְעַטִּים,

26.   וּטְמֵאִים בְּיַד טְהוֹרִים,

27.   וּרְשָׁעִים בְּיַד   צַדִּיקִים,

28.   וְזֵדִים בְּיַד עוֹסְקֵי

      תוֹרָתֶךָ.

29.   וּלְךָ עָשִׂיתָ שֵׁם גָּדוֹל

30.   וְקָדוֹשׁ בְּעוֹלָמֶךָ,

31.   וּלְעַמְּךָ יִשְׂרָאֵל

32.   עָשִׂיתָ תְּשׁוּעָה גְדוֹלָה

33.   וּפֻרְקָן כְּהַיּוֹם הַזֶּה.

34.   וְאַחַר כֵּן בָּאוּ בָנֶיךָ

35.   לִדְבִיר בֵּיתֶךָ

36.   וּפִנּוּ אֶת־הֵיכָלֶךָ

37.   וְטִהֲרוּ אֶת־מִקְדָּשֶׁךָ,

38.   וְהִדְלִיקוּ נֵרוֹת

39.   בְּחַצְרוֹת קָדְשֶׁךָ

40.   וְקָבְעוּ שְׁמוֹנַת יְמֵי

      חֲנֻכָּה אֵלּוּ,

41.   לְהוֹדוֹת וּלְהַלֵּל

42.   לְשִׁמְךָ הַגָּדוֹל.

MIRACLES

Jewish tradition includes a number of events which are beyond nature that we call "miracles." The parting of the Reed Sea, Joshua commanding the sun to stand still, manna falling in the desert, the giving of the Ten Commandments, the occurrence of the Ten Plagues, the collapse of the walls of Jericho, the burning bush that was not consumed, etc. One of the most famous of Jewish miracle stories is associated with Hanukkah—the single jug of oil lasting eight days instead of one. Though hardly central to Jewish belief and practice, these stories are often presented to our children. In fact, the "oil lasting eight days" story is what most people learned as the "reason" for celebrating Hanukkah, even though it clearly was a legend created by the rabbis to give religious meaning to a military event that occured hundreds of years earlier.

Nevertheless, the idea of miracles, especially as evidence of God's intervention in history, is an important part of the message of Hanukkah. How should we discuss miracles in the family?

Two factors will influence how we talk about miracles with our children and grandchildren: 1) the age of the child, and 2) your belief system. For young children, the miracle stories cause wide-eyed wonder and delight. The message of the miracles is that the innocent and the just are helped by God.

When the kids are older and the question arises, "How could it happen?," your theology will dictate an approach. If you believe in a God who, in fact, can intervene in history, then a traditional answer is that miracles are **above** human reason. We simply cannot understand them and we accept them on faith. Moreover, the morals underlying the miracles are what is most important.

If you do not believe that the miracles actually happened, you might want to include these ideas in your approach:

1. The Bible stories were written through the eyes of people who believed God could suspend the laws of Nature to help the Israelites.

2. Something important did happen in these miracles; by recalling the event in an exciting story, we are helped to remember it.

3. The stories are legends and/or metaphors and we can learn important lessons from them.

4. The miracle stories are telling us something crucial to a Jewish belief system: God is on the side of those who try to do right.

5. The miraculous events may, in fact, have been actual occurrences in Nature which were exaggerated in retelling because their timing was so important.

6. Today, and every day, "miraculous" things happen; e.g. recovery from major ill-ness, survival of Israel. We just describe them in different words. In the *Amidah*, we find the paragraph that begins *Modim anakhnu lakh...*—"We gratefully thank You..." In the prayer, we thank God for a number of things, among them *v'al nisekha sheh-b'khol yom imanu*—"for Your miracles that are with us every day." What a profound tradition that recognizes the daily miracles in life and thanks God for them three times a day!

See Harold S. Kushner, *When Children Ask About God*, Reconstructionist Press, New York, 1971, for more suggestions on how to talk with children about miracles.

8

The Hanukkah Gallery

We usually make cookies. We make Hanukkah cookies. We have special cookie cutters and we make regular cookies and we cut out the shapes with the cookie cutters and then we sprinkle them with blue and white sprinkles so they look Jewish.

Karen Bobrow

Although Hanukkah is not considered a major holiday in the Jewish calendar, a number of customs designed to enhance the celebration have evolved throughout the centuries. As we will discuss in Part II, the influence of Christmas has clearly motivated families to find ways to embellish the rather simple required ritual.

Food is central to any Jewish celebration. Traditional foods imbued with symbolism of the holiday became standard fare in Jewish homes throughout the world. Since the holiday comes in the dead of winter, games of chance became associated with the holiday, brightening up the otherwise long, dark nights. The singing of songs, both traditional hymns and modern children's tunes, has helped to increase the joy of the evening. And, certainly, the tradition of giving gifts at Hanukkah has become one of the most eagerly anticipated parts of most Hanukkah observances.

In this "Hanukkah Gallery," we present a number of ideas for joyous Hanukkah celebration.

THE MEAL

DEBBIE NEINSTEIN: I am the family Hanukkah lady. Everybody in the family has their holiday and I do Hanukkah. We will generally have all of my family and all of Larry's family. We have 50 people in our house.

YOUR AUTHOR: Every night?

DEBBIE NEINSTEIN: No. Usually the first night. We have tables set up in the living room, the dining room, and the kitchen and the den. We will have 20 menorahs going at once and it is really beautiful. One year, we had the most beautiful cake. My sister-in-law has a friend who makes cakes and she is very creative. This particular cake was a menorah and each candle was its own cake. It was on an enormous board and decorated beautifully with a different color for each "candle" and it was iced and with a flame on it. It was just beautiful.

HESTER COBLENS: I like the latkes, because they taste so good.

YOUR AUTHOR: What tastes so good about them? Why are they different? You have French fries and stuff. Aren't they sort of like latkes?

HESTER COBLENS: Latkes have a Jewish taste.

Unlike the meals of the three pilgrimage holidays—Sukkot, Passover, and Shavuot—or the meals of Shabbat, the Hanukkah meal is not considered a "*seudat mitzvah*," a commanded meal. For instance, there is no formal *Kiddush*, sanctification of the wine. Nevertheless, as the Hanukkah holiday has gained in importance, the evening meal of Hanukkah has become a special culinary experience.

The key ingredient in the Hanukkah meal is oil. Ashkenazic Jews adapted the popular potato pancake of Eastern Europe, creating *latkes* (*levivot* in Hebrew), perhaps the most famous of Hanukkah delicacies. Sephardic Jews fry jelly doughnuts (*sufganiyot* in Hebrew) for Hanukkah, now an important Hanukkah tradition in Israel. Both foods are fried in oil, reminding us of the oil used in the menorah of the Temple.

Cheese is the other traditional ingredient in Hanukkah meals. Recall that Judith fed Holofernes salty cheese to encourage him to drink wine, just before he was lulled to sleep, only to be dispatched by our heroine (see *The Book of Judith* 10:451). Many communities feature cheese dishes for Hanukkah. In Algeria, the children are given bread, cheese, and fruit for meals in school on Hanukkah. In some Sephardic enclaves, a special community dinner just for women is held featuring cheese dishes and wine.

Among other communities, different traditions arose. The Yemenites claim the Maccabees ate a carrot stew. In Hungary, people ate a garlic stew on the first day of Hanukkah, especially if the day fell close to Christmas! In Eastern Europe, most of the geese were slaughtered before Hanukkah since they were about as fat as they were going to get before the sparse winter. Some of the meat was salted and stored away. The rest made a festive meal for the holiday.

Whatever traditions you continue, here are some recipes for Hanukkah foods to eat at your celebration.

LATKES

TRADITIONAL POTATO LATKES

You'll need:
    12 large potatoes, grated
    3 medium onions, grated
    4 eggs, beaten lightly
    5 tbs. flour
    3 tsp. salt
    1 tsp. pepper
    Oil for deep frying

Here's how:

The secret to great latkes is to remove as much liquid from the potatoes and onions as possible. Put the grated potatoes in a clean tea towel and squeeze the liquid out of the mixture. Do the same for the grated onions. Combine all the ingredients and mix together well by hand.

In a heavy skillet, put a 3/4" deep layer of oil. Heat until sizzling. Form individual pancakes by hand and carefully slide into the pan using a slotted spatula. Fill the pan, but leave room between the pancakes. When the latkes are nicely browned on one side, turn carefully and cook until browned on the other side and crisp on the edges. Remove with a spatula and place on paper towels. Let the excess grease drain onto the paper towel. Serve immediately for the best taste. You can keep the latkes hot in a warm oven. Serve with sour cream or applesauce, or sprinkle with granulated sugar.

PATATOKEFTEDAKIA

(GREEK LATKES)

You'll need:
    1 lb. potatoes
    4 lbs. flour
    1 tbs. butter, melted
    1 tbs. each parsley and green onion, chopped fine
    2 cloves garlic, crushed
    Salt and pepper to taste
    Oil for deep frying

Here's how:

Boil the potatoes in their skins until they are soft. Run under cold water, peel the skins and refrigerate covered, until well-chilled. Run the cold potatoes through a sieve and add the melted butter, garlic, parsley, green onion, flour, salt and pepper. For best results, the pancakes should be highly peppered. Kneed the mixture lightly until it is smooth. Form into balls about 1 1/2 inch in diameter. Drop gently into the hot oil until golden brown.

APPLE LATKES

You'll need:
    2 large tart apples
    1 1/4 cup sugar
    1 1/2 cups flour
    1 tablespoon sugar
    1 teaspoon baking powder
    1/2 teaspoon salt
    1 egg, beaten
    1 cup milk
    1 tablespoon melted vegetable
        shortening
    pinch nutmeg
    oil for frying
    cinnamon sugar

Here's how:

Wash and core apples. Do not peel. Slice each apple into 12 thin slices. Sprinkle with sugar and let stand. Sift together flour, sugar, baking powder and salt into mixing bowl. Beat egg, milk, and melted shortening together and stir into dry mixture to form thin batter. Season with nutmeg. Heat a well-greased frying pan. Pour several large dollops of batter into the pan. Place a slice of apple in center of each spoonful and top with a second large dollop of batter, covering the apple. Fry over moderate heat until lightly browned, then turn to brown other side. Serve hot with sprinkling of cinnamon sugar.

SWEET POTATO LATKES

You'll need:
 1 large peeled sweet potato
 1 small onion
 2 large eggs
 2 tablespoons flour
 1/4 teaspoon ground cinnamon
 3 tablespoons oil
 salt and pepper to taste

Here's how:

Use your food processor to shred the potato and onion. Place in colander to squeeze out as much moisture as possible. Transfer to a mixing bowl and stir. Quickly process the eggs, flour, cinnamon, salt and pepper until mixed thoroughly. Stir the egg-flour mixture into the sweet potato-onion mixture. Heat the oil in a medium frying pan over medium heat. Drop the mixture by the tablespoon into the hot oil. Sweet potato latkes cook for one minute on each side, or until lightly browned.

TUNA LATKES

You'll need:
 2—7 oz. cans of water-packed tuna
 2/3 cup chopped onions
 2 eggs
 1/2 cup matzo meal
 oil
 salt and pepper to taste

Here's how:

Place tuna and its liquid in a mixing bowl. Add onion, eggs, matzo meal, salt and pepper. Mix well. Let stand 15 minutes. Moisten your hands and shape mixture into latkes. Fry in hot oil over medium-high heat until golden brown on both sides. Drain on paper towels. Can be served hot or cold. Makes a dozen latkes.

CARROTY POTATO LATKES

You'll need:
 Water
 Juice of one lemon
 4-5 medium white rose (thin-skinned) potatoes
 6 eggs
 1/2 cup flour
 3 cups shredded carrots (approx. 4 medium)
 1 1/2 teaspoon light salt
 1/4 teaspoon pepper
 1 medium onion, chopped
 2 cloves garlic, pressed
 1/2 cup oil

Here's how:

Fill a large bowl half-full with cold water and the lemon juice. Using food processor, shred potatoes and keep immersed in lemony water to prevent discoloration during preparation. Then shred carrots and onion. Set aside. Beat until smooth: the eggs, flour, salt and pepper. Stir in onion, garlic, carrots and potatoes—and your batter is ready!

In a large skillet, heat safflower oil over medium-high heat. Pour batter into hot oil and flatten into oval-shaped cakes. Fry for 3-4 minutes on each side until golden and crisp, adding more oil as needed. Drain latkes on paper towels and keep warm in a 200 degree oven until all are fried and ready to eat. Serve with applesauce or sour cream. Makes 16 latkes.

MARSHMALLOW DREIDLES

For each dreidle you'll need:
    1 kosher marshmallow
    1 chocolate candy kiss
    1 3" licorice stick
    Icing

Here's how:

Assemble dreidle by pushing the licorice stick through the marshmallow and attaching the kiss to the bottom of the marshmallow using icing as "glue." Write the letters "nun," "gimmel," "hei," and "shin" on each side of the marshmallow with the icing.

HANUKKAH DOUGH BALLS

You'll need:
    1 cup apple juice
    4 oz. margarine (1 stick)
    1 cup flour
    4 eggs
    Oil for frying

Here's how:

Boil apple juice and add margarine stirring until melted. Keeping the pan on the burner, add flour until mixture forms a ball and doesn't stick to the sides of the pan. Remove from burner and beat in eggs one at a time. Heat the oil in a deep fryer, wok, or large frying pan. Once oil is hot, the dough can be dropped by teaspoons into the hot oil. Fry until golden brown making sure that the dough balls puff and are cooked evenly. Remove from oil with strainer and drain on paper towels. Serve hot with assorted dips: cinnamon sugar, powdered sugar, heated raspberry preserves, hot chocolate sauce, hot honey and chopped nuts, heated marmalade with shredded coconut.

PONTSHKES (*SUFGANIYOT*—HANUKKAH DOUGHNUTS)

You'll need:
    1 package dry yeast
    3/4 cup lukewarm milk
    2 tablespoons sugar
    Pinch salt
    2 1/2 cups flour
    2 egg yolks or 1 whole egg
    2 teaspoons cinnamon
    5 teaspoons melted margarine
    1 cup jam
    1/2 cup confectioner's sugar
    Oil for deep frying

Here's how:

Dissolve the yeast in the warm milk. Add sugar and salt. Set aside to rise. Sift the flour—make a well and add yeast mixture, eggs, and cinnamon. Knead the dough and add the melted margarine. Continue kneading until the dough stops sticking to your hands. Let rise in a warm place until it doubles in size.

Turn out the dough on a floured board and roll to 1/4 inch thickness. Cut into circles with floured doughnut cutter or thin-rimmed glass. Place a teaspoon of your favorite kind of jam in center of every second circle. Press a plain circle on top and let stand for 20 minutes.

Drop four or five at a time into hot oil. Fry until golden brown. Turn doughnuts as they rise to surface and fry for one minute more. Drain and sprinkle with confectioner's sugar or shake in bag containing confectioner's sugar.

GAMES

I remember my father used to take hazelnuts and line them up near the wall and flick a nut and it would hit another nut and they would bash against the wall. He told me that he learned it as a kid in Brooklyn because they were too poor to get presents for Hanukkah. I remember sitting on the kitchen floor and playing that game. Now, in my family, we take a *s'vivon* and we have hazelnuts as the gambling chips.

Debbie Neinstein

GAMES

One of the most interesting aspects of Hanukkah is the playing of games. From the earliest days of the holiday, games have been a customary part of the celebration. Some scholars conjecture that games of luck became attached to Hanukkah to reflect the "luck" of the victorious Maccabees. Others point to the need for amusements to pass away the long evenings of the midwinter season. Whatever the reason, games have become an important part of any Hanukkah celebration.

DREIDLE

Although normally frowned upon, games of chance emerged as the most popular of the games of Hanukkah. The best known of these involves a spinning top, called a *dreidle* (Yiddish) or *s'vivon* (Hebrew). On each of the four sides of the dreidle is one of four Hebrew letters: *nun, gimmel, hey, shin.* The letters are the initials of the words *"Nes gadol hayah sham,"* literally, "A great miracle happened there." Of course, this refers to the miracle of the victorious Maccabees that happened "there," in the land of Israel. In fact, an Israeli *s'vivon* will have a letter *"pey"* instead of a *"shin,"* for the corresponding phrase in Israel is *"Nes gadol hayah poh,"* "A great miracle happened **here.**"

The game of dreidle is played in any number of variations. The most popular follows these rules:

1.   Every player puts in an equal share of something—nuts, raisins, pennies, candy Hanukkah coins—into the "pot."

      (See "Susie's Gelt Surprise" for an exciting alternative.)

2.   The first player takes a turn spinning the dreidle. Depending on which letter is showing on the dreidle when it lands, the player does the following:

      Nun נ : *(Nisht)* Neither get nor put; Nothing

      Gimmel ג : *(Gantz)* Get everything (then start a new "pot")

      Heh ה : *(Halb)* get Half the pot

      Shin ש : *(Shtel)* Shell out; put more in the pot—whatever number was agreed to at the beginning of play

3. Play proceeds clockwise around the circle of players, each person taking a turn. When a *Gimmel* lands and the pot is taken, each player puts another share into the pot.

4. The winner is determined when one player has won all the goodies from the other players. Or, the game is called when the latkes are ready!

SUSIE'S GELT SURPRISE

As our kids grew older, the dreidle game lost some of its appeal. So, Susie devised an exciting element that has brought them back to the dreidle game year after year.

She took a dozen whole walnuts and split them in half. This is not easy to do; use a sharp-pointed knife to ease the two half shells apart. Once split open, she dug all the nut meat out from inside of the shell. Then, she put either a penny, a nickle, a dime, a quarter, or a folded-up dollar bill inside one side of the shell. Using super glue, Susie then closed the shell by attaching the other side. She mixed up these special walnuts with regular ones and divided them among the dreidle players. Of course, only Susie knew the real value of the walnuts used during the game. After a ten-minute time limit, the game was declared over and Susie announced that there was a special surprise in the walnuts. She distributed nutcrackers and the players opened the nuts they had left at the end of the game, revealing the Hanukkah gelt inside the shells. What excitement! It turned out that even those with just a few nuts in their possession at the end of the game often "won" more Hanukkah gelt than those with more nuts.

GEMATRIA

When stodgy folks objected to the playing of dreidle, the ever-resourceful pointed to a favorite mystical exercise known as "*gematria*" to show the importance of the dreidle. In *gematria*, each Hebrew letter has a numeric equivalent. For example, *alef* = 1, *bet* = 2, etc. The numerical equivalents of the letters on the dreidle are:

nun	=	50
gimmel	=	3
hey	=	5
shin	=	300
		358

Remarkably, this is equivalent to the exact numerical value for the word *"mashiah"*—Messiah.

mem	=	40
shin	=	300
yud	=	10
het	=	8
		358

Thus, playing dreidle was permitted because it allowed concentration on bringing the Messiah!

In a variation of the dreidle game, the person who can make the top spin the longest, wins. Or, the game can be scored by using the numerical equivalents above, and so the first person to 1,000, wins.

Another well-known Hanukkah diversion is wordplays. For example, three important words related to Hanukkah all share the same three letters: *shin*, *mem*, and *nun*. Oil = *SheMeN*, Eight = *SheMoNah*, Hasmoneans = *HaShMoNim*.

> What's the connection between latkes and love?
>
> The latke usually forms the shape of the heart, the Hebrew word for heart is *lev*.
>
> The Hebrew word for latke is *levivot*, and Hanukkah comes in the month of *Kis-lev*.

Judah was called "Maccabee." Various suggestions have been made as to what Maccabee means. *Makkev* in Hebrew means "hammer," a reference to the strength of Judah the soldier. It is said that one of the popular slogans of the Maccabean War was *Mi Khamokha Ba-elim Adonai*, "Who is like you, Adonai, among the gods?" The first letters spell *MaKaBEe*. And, the last letters of the names of the three fathers of the Jewish people are AbrahaM, IsaaC, and JacoB.

What is the significance of the word Hanukkah? It literally means "dedication," referring to the rededication of the Temple by the Maccabees. The word *hanu* means "they rested" and *kah* stands for *kaf* and *hei* which numerically add up to 25, so "they rested on the 25th" day of Kislev.

OTHER GAMES

Other ideas for Hanukkah diversions include transforming board games into Hanukkah games. For example, chess and checkers can feature opposing Maccabees and Syrian-Greeks. A *Scrabble*™ variation awards bonus points for words related to

Hanukkah. Hide and seek or treasure hunts with Hanukkah gelt can recall the Maccabees hiding in caves.

GIFTS

In past years, everybody gave everybody else presents. It really got completely out of control. So, this year when we have all the families together, each family will give to their own children and grandchildren, not to everyone else's children, too. Jack's sister will give to her grandchildren. We'll give to our grandchildren. And the parents will give to their kids. That way we hope to keep it from being more like Christmas than Christmas. It should feel like Hanukkah, not Christmas.

Rae Gindi

HANUKKAH GELT

Savings bonds, checks, and small chocolate coins wrapped in gold foil—these are the modern incarnations of the traditional gift known as Hanukkah gelt. "Gelt" is a Yiddish term for "money." Although it is an old and cherished custom, the roots of gelt-giving go back much further than the Middle Ages, the era in which the custom is usually said to have originated. Although it is mentioned in neither the Talmud nor the *Shulḥan Arukh* (the Code of Jewish Law), the importance of coins in the history of the Hasmonean period is undeniable.

The First Book of Maccabees records that in 142 B.C.E., 22 years after the Temple was recaptured, Simon the Maccabee, the surviving son of Mattathias, finally brought independence to Judea. Syria's King Antiochus VII declared to Simon: "I turn over to you the right to make your own stamp for coinage for your country." (*I Maccabees* 15:6) The ability to mint its own coins was a concrete expression of the newly-won independence of the Jewish people.

During the following years of the Hasmonean dynasty, the first Jewish coins in history were issued. Most depicted cornucopia, symbolic of the prosperity of the country during these years. One of the coins minted by the last of the Hasmonean kings, Antigonus Matityahu (40-37 B.C.E.), portrayed the seven-branched menorah on one side and the Table of Shew Bread on the other, both symbols of the restored Temple. Some scholars conjecture that these designs may actually have been intended to remind the people of Hanukkah, which had been neglected during the waning years of the Hasmonean dynasty.

When the Second Temple was destroyed in 70 C.E., Jewish coinage ceased until modern times, except for a brief period during the Bar Kochba Revolution (132-135 C.E.). So, no Jewish coins were available to distribute when the custom of Hanukkah gelt-giving emerged as an important part of the festival during the Middle Ages. Then, it was traditional to give Hanukkah gelt to the local Jewish teacher; in fact, it was his primary means of support. When the tradition was expanded to include giving coins to children, it became a way to emphasize the importance of Jewish education and the study of Torah.

Since the founding of the State of Israel, Jewish coinage has become a fascinating part of numismatics world-wide. In 1958, the Bank of Israel initiated a program of striking special commemorative coins for use as Hanukkah gelt. In a brilliantly conceived move to link the modern world with the ancient history of our people, the first Hanukkah coin portrayed exactly the same menorah that had appeared on the last Maccabean coins of Antigonus Matityahu, 1,998 years earlier. Each year since 1958 (except 1964-71), the Hanukkah gelt coin has honored a different Jewish community around the world. In 1972, a silver coin was struck showing a 20th century Russian menorah, a rather clear message to the world about Soviet Jewry. On the 200th anniversary of the United States' Declaration of Independence, the 1976 Hanukkah coin featured a colonial American menorah. Other issues through the years have featured *hanukkiyot* from many different lands where Jews have lived.

Consider buying some Bank of Israel Hanukkah gelt. It is a terrific and traditional Hanukkah gift, it is a wonderful way to start a meaningful coin collection, and the coins themselves appreciate in value. Most importantly, your dollars help the State of Israel.

The coins come in two versions: Brilliant Uncirculated and Proof. They cost between $15 and $50, depending on the year. The State of Israel Hanukkah gelt can be acquired from two Israeli government authorized coin importers:

J.J. Van Grover
P.O.B. 123
Oakland Gardens, New York 11364
(718) 224-9578

PandaAmerica
23326 Hawthorne Boulevard, Suite 150
Torrance, California 90505
(213) 373-9647

or contact the nearest Israeli consulate for information.

Whatever your source for Hanukkah gelt, it is always a wonderful tradition to put some of what you receive into a *tzedakah* box in order to share your good fortune with those in need or for a good cause.

The process of buying and giving gifts is a remarkable phenomenon at any time, but especially during the Hanukkah season. That the stores are stocked to the ceiling with gift items, often pre-wrapped for a quick purchase, or that the media are bursting with advertisements touting the virtues of this gift or that gift goes without saying. But, one's approach to the buying, giving and receiving of gifts reflects a set of values that are not unimportant.

1. THE LIST

"The List" is undoubtedly a cultural borrowing from the other winter holiday, but has become an important part of Hanukkah preparation. In many homes, there are two Lists: The List of presents each child hopes to get and The List of presents the parent(s) intend(s) to buy. The first list, often called the Hanukkah Wish List, is compiled formally or informally, usually in response to grandparents and other relatives who call to inquire about what _____ wants for Hanukkah. Sometimes The List is filled with generalities—a bicycle, music tapes, money. Sometimes The List is quite specific—a Super Mario Brothers II Nintendo game, a Beach Bunny Barbie, a 1986 Jose Canseco rookie baseball card, Donruss.

The second List, the Hanukkah Reality List, consists of those items parents have compiled from all the Wish Lists and that they think they are capable of acquiring this year. Oftentimes, items on this List get allocated to grandparents and other relatives looking for gift ideas. But, in the end, these are the gifts that will make up the Hanukkah booty for any particular year.

2. THE POLICY

"The Policy" refers to a family's particular gift-giving practices. Many families have what can be called the "One Night Big Gift" Policy. Family members get one "big gift" on one night of Hanukkah, usually the first night, sometimes the last night, or, depending on when the family gathers, sometimes at the big family Hanukkah celebration. On the other nights of the holiday, small gifts are given, if any. Other families have the "Eight Nights, Eight Gifts" Policy. The presents are piled up in front of the *hanukkiyah* and each person gets to choose which present (s)he will open on each night. If there are more than eight presents, a number of gifts might be opened during the first evenings of Hanukkah.

Our family policy has followed this latter suggestion. Of course, the kids are truly funny as they approach the difficult decision of which present to open. They size up and shake the boxes, guessing (usually correctly) which box contains a "big" gift, a game, or (yuk) new clothes. Hints are requested from parents and siblings about which gift is likely to result in the most excitement.

The other policy in place at the Wolfson homestead is "no presents until after candle-lighting." This makes for quick blessings and even briefer singing of *Maoz Tzur* and the like. The instant the songs are done, the pile of presents is attacked.

Inevitably, as the days of Hanukkah go by, the pile of presents gets smaller and smaller. Yet, when offered alternative gift-giving procedures, our kids demur. I know they appreciate the power to choose which gift will be opened. And, remarkably, they parcel out their presents to cover the eight nights quite equitably.

Actually, Hanukkah is **not** the traditional time for gift-giving in the Jewish calendar. Purim, with its "*mishloah manot,*" the sending of presents, is historically the holiday for gift exchanges. Yet, due undeniably to the influence of Christmas and its commercialization, gift-giving has become a major part of the modern Hanukkah celebration.

The Coblens' family tradition of dedicating each night to a different type of gift is not unusual. Here's another suggestion for a Hanukkah gift-giving plan:

First night: "Big gift night" (parents give to children)

Second night: "Parent night" (children give to parents)

Third night: "Grandparent Night" (children give to grandparent[s])

Fourth night: "Poem night" (everyone recites an original poem)

Fifth night: "Small gift night" (parents give to children)

Sixth night: "Gift of Self Night" (non-monetary gift from each person to another or to the entire family)

Seventh night: "Giving Night" (everyone gives a gift to a charity of his/her choosing, with the children's gifts matched by the parents)

Eighth Night: "Word night" (a game in which each person tries to stump the others with difficult words)

Most gifts have a very short life-span. They are used for a few days, a few weeks, and then end up in a closet or on a shelf, rarely to be used again. Here are ten "presents with a future:"

1. Assemble a family photo album

2. Open a Hanukkah savings account for a future trip to Israel.

3. Take a formal family portrait.

4.   Tape an oral family history as a living legacy for the future.

5.   Start a stamp or coin collection (perhaps with a Ḥanukkah gelt coin from Israel)

6.   Purchase necessities for an indoor/outdoor perennial garden.

7.   Present each child with his/her own *ḥanukkiyah*. This is how family heirlooms are created.

8.   Start a family scrapbook.

9.   Buy Israel bonds.

10. Expand a Jewish record, tape, CD, or book library.

3. GIFT EXCHANGES

Many families and friends gather together for Ḥanukkah parties and a major moment of the event is a gift exchange. More than one Ḥanukkah party has come to a crashing halt because a child was left out or unhappy about his/her end of the exchange, especially when there is an indiscriminate "grab-bag."

Our *ḥavurah* has an annual Ḥanukkah party, complete with candlelighting, Ḥanukkah songs, Maccabee parades, decorations, latkes, *sufganiyot*, and...a gift exchange. At the *ḥavurah* meeting just before our Ḥanukkah party, we place the name of every child in the *ḥavurah* on a slip of paper, put the slips in a sack, and each family picks the number of names corresponding to the number of children in their family. For example, the Inlanders have three kids, so they would pick three names. They will be responsible for buying gifts for the three children on the slips. We limit the value of each gift to less than $10. Then, at the party, each child gets a gift that is age-appropriate. Another solution is to have each family bring one gift for each of their children to open at the party.

Decorations

I remember making those dreidles of marshmallows and Hershey kisses and we would go to assemblies and that is all I remember...Then we had latkes and we made a circle and they gave us *sufganiyot* and I think we played dreidle.

Alissa Bobrow

We were into Styrofoam decorations, like forty or fifty of these Styrofoam decorations, like dreidles, like Torahs, like Maccabees with glitter. These huge decorations with glitter. The other thing that we did is like a real no-no. We had a "Hanukkah Star," not a tree. It was a big *Magen David* wrapped in tin foil. It was this tall and about so wide. That's where we put the presents.

Larry Neinstein

There is no historical evidence that Jews decorated their homes for Hanukkah. Clearly, the idea of decorations is borrowed from the observance of Christmas. Yet, the spirit of decorating the home is in keeping with the general tone of the holiday—to bring joy into an otherwise dark and dreary home during the midwinter solstice.

While some families abhor the idea of Hanukkah decorations, many others find that brightening the home with arts and crafts, homemade or store-bought, adds to the observance of the holiday. Decorating is certainly not *against* Jewish law, although one might be cautioned against excessive use of commercially made decorations. On the one hand, use of blue and white lights, silver tinsel, and other Christmas-like decorations marketed as Hanukkah decor might be offensive to some. On the other hand, putting up handmade decorations your children or grandchildren make in religious school will certainly add to the joy of the holiday.

Ultimately, the use of decorations is a question of taste. Each person, each family will feel differently about the issue. Once again, the point is clear. The "art" of Jewish living is in knowing the basic components of Jewish practice. How we compose our "pictures" of Jewish observance in the family is up to each of us.

ELKE COBLENS:	I remember having a set of stencils that you would put up on the windows. I looked for one for my kids one time, but I don't know if I ever found it. I suppose it's a little like window decorations for Christmas; one of the early take-offs or adaptations of Christmas decorations. It had a Jewish star, a menorah and a Judah Maccabee. I remember doing that on the front windows, I think. I could picture where we lit the *hanukkiyah*. It was not in front of the window the way we do it now.
YOUR AUTHOR:	Where did you get those pretty decorations?
DAVID BOBROW:	I don't know, my Mom buys them usually.
CLAUDIA BOBROW:	We have accumulated them over the years.
SHLOMO BOBROW:	Some of them we buy every year.
YOUR AUTHOR:	Where do you keep them when it is not Hanukkah?
DAVID BOBROW:	In boxes in the garage.
YOUR AUTHOR:	And what about your *hanukkiyot*, where do they go?

DAVID BOBROW: In the garage. We have this big dreidle that my Mom made out of a cardboard box. We put all of our Hanukkah stuff in there and we store it in the garage.

JONATHAN KIRSCH: This is a tapestry that was made by my late grandmother who was a seamstress. She had a great talent. She also made the *huppah* that we were married under. My step-father lettered it. We put it up every year for Hanukkah.

YOUR AUTHOR: That is beautiful.

JONATHAN KIRSCH: We have decorations all around the house, but this to me is like a family heirloom.

The New Jewish Arts

We are living during a renaissance of Jewish art. The variety and quality of Jewish artisans creating beautiful expressions of Jewish themes in a number of media is truly astounding. While once dependent on the "green glob" menorahs of a generation ago, today's Jewish families have a wide range of truly lovely ritual objects with which to fill their home.

Judaism has always striven for egalitarianism in required ritual objects. A plain candle-holder can serve as well as silver candlesticks, a simple glass as a Kiddush cup. Nevertheless, throughout the centuries, Jewish artisans have viewed ritual objects as appropriate subjects for their creativity. This is, in part, because of a long-held prohibition against depicting human or divine forms in Jewish art. But, it is also due to the concept of *hiddur mitzvah*, the embellishment of a commandment. According to this idea, we are to strive to enhance the celebration of an obligation by beautifying our homes, our ceremonies, and our ritual objects. Thus, on Shabbat, our dinner is served on white linens, using fine china, and featuring special foods.

Whatever the reasons, those searching for Hanukkah objects have a wide selection from which to choose. Ranging from the innovative painted ceramic *hanukkiyot* of Robert Lipnick to the gorgeous silver dreidles of H. Braginsky, the opportunity to enhance a family's collection of beautiful Jewish ritual items with original Jewish art becomes readily apparent upon a visit to any Jewish gift shop offering quality Jewish art. And, for those who live in smaller Jewish communities where the selection is not as comprehensive, there are Jewish gift catalogs from merchants who offer quality ritual objects by mail.

HOMEMADE HANUKKAH

Of course, there is nothing quite as precious as a handmade *hanukkiyah*, fashioned in a Jewish religious school. Havi and Michael routinely brought home wonderfully creative *hanukkiyot* each year from their Jewish preschools. One featured two metal nuts glued on top of each other to form the candleholders; another used round Tinker Toy™ pieces with holes in the middle. Perhaps the most dramatic of these masterpieces was the *hanukkiyah* fashioned from the handles of jump ropes. Nine handles in a row, with little round discs glued on the front to form a shield—a little face drawn in and *voila*, a Maccabee Warrior *Hanukkiyah*!

The important point to be made about these creations is that they should be **used** when brought home. Even if you have invested in a major piece of Jewish ritual art for your family *hanukkiyah*, the importance of the message sent to young children when their own handmade *hanukkiyot* are used for kindling the Hanukkah lights cannot be overstated. In fact, many families save each handmade *hanukkiyah*, adding it to their collections, and using them all every year.

In addition to *hanukkiyot*, children will often bring home Hanukkah decorations made in school. Use them to decorate your Hanukkah candlelighting center or around the house. Save them from year to year and enjoy the growing collection of cut-out menorahs, dreidles, "stained glass" windows, and whatever else resourceful teachers have children make in class for Hanukkah.

For the creative types among our readers, we have included some terrific Hanukkah arts and crafts projects for you to do with your children.

Hanukkah Crafts

HANUKKAH CRYSTAL CRAFTS

Here's a quick and easy art project for the whole family! We know you'll enjoy creating your own durable and beautiful Hanukkah decorations.

Begin with Plastic Baking Crystals (available at craft and hobby stores) and open metal cookie cutters and cake molds shaped in the form of holiday symbols—Stars of David, dreidles, *hanukkiyot*, candles, elephants, and the like.

You'll need to place the metal forms on top of foil or aluminum cookie sheets. Follow the baking decorations on the package of crystals. Try to dabble a bit with color and special effects. Be sure to poke a hole in each crystal craft item while they are still warm, for easy hanging later.

Once the crystals are baked, insert fishing line thread for the invisible hanging look. Place your decorations in front of windows so that the sunlight can play with the colors, thus spreading the rays of Hanukkah joy throughout your home. And, don't forget to preserve your crystal crafts for next Hanukkah.

HANUKKAH COUNTDOWN CALENDAR, OR, *BEIT* SHAMMAI'S REVENGE

Younger children are especially eager to know how many days of Hanukkah remain. Here is a hands-on calendar you can make with your young person to help count down the days.

You'll need:
The bottom part of a shoebox
Hanukkah pictures from greeting cards, gift wrap, etc.
Construction paper
Markers
Glue
Scissors
8 spring-type clothespins

Here's how:

Begin by decorating the shoebox with the Hanukkah pictures, gift wrap, cut-outs, and original drawings of Hanukkah symbols. Label each clothespin with consecutive numbers, or with Hebrew letters, or with specific dates. Have the younger children clip the clothespins around the box's edge. Have a daily countdown by removing one clothespin each day of Hanukkah.

STARMALLOW MOBILE

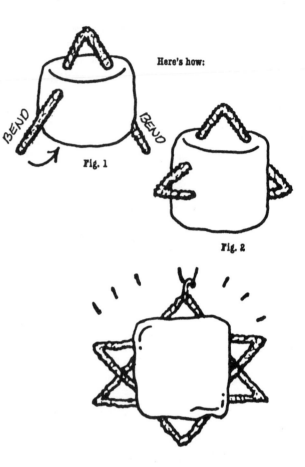

Fig. 1

Fig. 2

You'll need:

    1 large kosher marshmallow
    2 blue pipe cleaners
    Yarn or fishing wire

Step 1:   Bend one pipe cleaner in half and drive the ends through the top right and left corners of the marshmallow.

    (See Figure 1)

Step 2:   Then bend the 2 ends and drive them through the marshmallow to complete a triangular shape.

    (See Figure 2)

Step 3:   When these steps are completed, turn the marshmallow upside down and repeat steps 1 and 2 with the second pipe cleaner.

Step 4:   Attach yarn or string to the top and hang with pride.

Variation: Make several Starmallows and hang at different lengths from the bottom of a wire coat hanger.

FUTUREMOBILES

As your family lights the _hanukkiyah_, take the time to dedicate each night's candle to improving the future of your Jewish identity. For example, on the first night of Hanukkah, after blessing and lighting the candle, talk to each other about ways you can enhance the future of your Jewish education. On the second night, discuss things you can do to make a brighter future for your synagogue; the third night—your family, and so on throughout the holiday.

Each family member should make a personal pledge.

Make a Futuremobile to represent these pledges in a creative home decoration for Hanukkah.

Pre-cut 8 candle shapes for each family member. Using construction paper or cardboard, have each family member write his/her dedication nightly and then hang with paper-clips as attachments onto a central wire coat hanger covered in foil or tinsel. Add a "candle" nightly.

"Future" Subjects:

1. My Jewish Education
2. My Synagogue
3. My Family
4. My Pledge to Judaism
5. My Pledge to Myself
6. My Jewish Community
7. My Pledge to Peace
8. My Pledge to Israel

HANUKKAH VALUES LINE

Cut out 8 dreidle shapes from construction paper. In large lettering, write one of the following eight value words on each dreidle cut-out:

1. Loving
2. Fun
3. Caring
4. Togetherness
5. Helping
6. Sharing
7. Learning
8. Jewish

String fishing line or yarn above your *hanukkiyah* candlelighting center. Each night, dedicate one candle to a family value, by discussing how that value is acted upon in your family. List 3-4 ideas on the dreidle-shape. Clip the dreidle onto the fishing line using a clothespin or paper clip.

MAIL-A-HANUKKAH

Here's a great craft that will make a terrific Hanukkah present for college kids and other faraway friends or relatives.

Choose a durable cardboard box that allows for compartments to house party items. Include things that reflect your recipient's personality and tastes. Be sure to include Hanukkah napkins, plastic utensils, paper goods, Hanukkah decorations, a *hanukkiyah*, a box of Hanukkah candles, matches, a dreidle, and some Hanukkah gelt. Decorate a 36-inch square of fabric for a linen tablecloth, using potato prints or holiday cookie cutters dipped in paint.

Pack the box with several inches of crumpled newspapers on the bottom so the contents won't rattle. Use blue, white, and yellow colored tissues as packing between items. Then tie the corners of the fabric tablecloth in the center. Write a special Hanukkah greeting and send your "Mail-a-Hanukkah" to someone you love!

Songs

I only remember one *hanukkiyah*. I remember it being referred to as a menorah. We would light it and then sing some songs.

Elke Coblens

Music is an important part of most Jewish celebrations, and Hanukkah is no exception. Popular Hanukkah songs are sung as part of the candlelighting ceremony and during the games and gift exchanges that are characteristic of Hanukkah evenings at home.

Even classical music has its Hanukkah diversion. *Judas Maccabeus,* by G. F. Handel, is often sung by choirs at Hanukkah time. Sometimes, the piece is performed as an "open sing" where spectators can join in the experience.

In some communities, performers and groups for children and families have developed Hanukkah shows. Puppeteers, singers, and a variety of other performers present the Hanukkah story in prose and song for children young and old. Give your family a wonderful Hanukkah gift by attending a Hanukkah show.

In the meantime, brush up the vocal cords, put in the cassette tape created for this book or any of the other tapes of holiday songs, and join your family in a spirited round of Hanukkah singing.

Hanukkah Songs

OH, HANUKKAH

Oh Hanukkah, Oh Hanukkah,
Come light the menorah.
Let's have a party,
We'll all dance the hora.
Gather round the table,
We'll give you a treat.
S'vivon to play with,
Latkes to eat.
And while we are playing
The candles are burning low.
One for each night,
They shed a sweet light,
To remind us of days long ago;
One for each night,
They shed a sweet light,
To remind us of days long ago.

OY HANUKKAH

Oy Hanukkah, Oy Hanukkah,
A yontef a sheiner,
A lustiger a freilicher
Nishto noch azoiner;
Alle nach in dredlach
Shpielen mir,
Zidik heise latkes
Es ohn a shier.
Tsint kinder,
Geshvinder,
Die dininke lichtelach ohn.
Zogt "Al HaNissim"
Loibt Gott far die nissim,
Und kumt gicher tanzen in kohn.
Zogt "Al HaNissim"
Loibt Gtt far die nissim,
Und kumt gicher tanzen in kohn.

NER LI

Ner li, ner li,	My candle, my candle,	נֵר לִי, נֵר לִי
Ner li dakik.	My little candle.	נֵר לִי דַקִיק.
Ba-Hanukkah	On Hanukkah	בַּחֲנֻכָּה
Neri adlik.	I will light my candle.	נֵרִי אַדְלִיק.
Ba-Hanukkah	On Hanukkah	בַּחֲנֻכָּה
Neri ya-ir,	My candle will glow,	נֵרִי יָאִיר
Ba-Hanukkah	On Hanukkah	בַּחֲנֻכָּה
Shirim ashir.	I will sing songs.	שִׁירִים אָשִׁיר.
Ba-Hanukkah	On Hanukkah	בַּחֲנֻכָּה
Neri ya-ir,	My candle will glow,	נֵרִי יָאִיר
Ba-Hanukkah	On Hanukkah	בַּחֲנֻכָּה
Shirim ashir	I will sing songs.	שִׁירִים אָשִׁיר.

I HAVE A LITTLE DREIDLE

I have a little dreidle,
I made it out of clay.
And when it's dry and ready,
Then dreidle I shall play.

(Chorus)

Oh dreidle, dreidle, dreidle,
I made it out of clay;
And when it's dry and ready,
Then dreidle I shall play.

It has a lovely body,
With leg so short and thin.
And when it gets all tired,
It drops and then I win.

(Chorus)

S'VIVON SOV, SOV, SOV

סְבִיבוֹן סֹב סֹב סֹב   חֲנֻכָּה הוּא חַג טוֹב
חֲנֻכָּה הוּא חַג טוֹב   סְבִיבוֹן סֹב סֹב סֹב
חַג שִׂמְחָה הוּא לָעָם נֵס גָּדוֹל הָיָה שָׁם
נֵס גָּדוֹל הָיָה שָׁם חַג שִׂמְחָה הוּא לָעָם

S'vivon, sov, sov, sov!	Dreidle, spin, spin, spin!
Hanukkah, hu ḥag tov;	Hanukkah is a good holiday;
Hanukkah, hu ḥag tov;	Haunkkah is a good holiday;
S'vivon, sov, sov, sov.	Dreidle, spin, spin, spin!
Hag simḥa hu la-am	It's a happy holiday for the people,
Nes gadol haya sham;	A great miracle happened there
Nes gadol haya sham;	A great miracle happened there
Hag simḥa hu la-am.	It's a happy holiday for the people.

(Repeat first stanza)

Words: Levin Kipnis
Music: N. Varsano

MI Y'MALEIL

מִי יְמַלֵּל גְּבוּרוֹת יִשְׂרָאֵל,

אוֹתָן מִי יִמְנֶה?

הֵן בְּכָל דּוֹר יָקוּם הַגִּבּוֹר,

גּוֹאֵל הָעָם

שְׁמַע! בַּיָּמִים הָהֵם בַּזְּמַן הַזֶּה

מַכַּבִּי מוֹשִׁיעַ וּפוֹדֶה.

וּבְיָמֵינוּ כָּל עַם יִשְׂרָאֵל

יִתְאַחֵד יָקוּם לְהִגָּאֵל!

(Chorus)
Mi y'maleil g'vurot Yisrael
Otan mi yimneh?
Hein b'khol dor yakum ha-gibor
Go-eil ha-am.

(Repeat chorus)

Sh'ma! Ba-yamim ha-heim
Ba-z'man ha-zeh.
Makabi moshiyah u-fodeh.
Uv'yameinu kol am Yisrael,
Yit'ahed yakum l'hi-ga-el.

(Repeat chorus)

Who can retell the things that befell them,
Who can count them?
In every age, a hero or sage
came to our aid.

Hark! In days of yore
In Israel's ancient land.
Brave Maccabeus led the faithful band.
But now all Israel must as one arise,
Redeem itself through deed and sacrifice.

Words and music: M. Ravina

PART II
The December Dilemmas

If H̲anukkah had happened in July instead of December, it would have made things a whole lot easier.

Claudia Bobrow

THE NEW REALITY

"Oh Hanukkah, oh Hanukkah,
Come light the menorah.
Let's have a party,
We'll all dance the hora."

Hanukkah Folk Song

"'Tis the season to be jolly,
Fa, la, la, la, la,
La, la, la, la."

Christmas Carol

For many Jews, December is the season of confusion—confusion brought on by the annual confrontation with an undeniable fact of Jewish life in North America: we are in the minority.

There are many more Christians than Jews. Our governments, both American and Canadian, were founded by Christians. The public school systems are much more likely to recognize Christian holidays. To the extent that the consumer economies of which we are a part are influenced by religious celebrations, Christian holidays are far more significant than Jewish holidays.

Thus, when December rolls around each year, nearly all Jews living on the North American continent must contend with the fact that, fortunately or unfortunately, Christmas and Hanukkah occur during the same season.

What are the questions raised by the so-called "December Dilemma?" What is the "dilemma" referred to? And what are we to do about it?

The first use of the term "December Dilemma" appears in articles written by rabbis in the mid-1950's when it became apparent that Jews were facing difficulties dealing with the ever-increasing presence of Christmas in their lives. Most of the advice in these articles revolved around the need to encourage Jews to resist the transformation of a religious holiday into a secular celebration. Or, they offered suggestions on how to cope with Christmas celebrations in the public schools which, in those days, 95% of Jewish children attended.

But, these advice columns all treated the problem from a certain distance. They were written with the assumption that the problem of Christmas was mostly an issue of confronting a foreign holiday "out there," in the public arena.

Certainly, there were some cautions against the introduction of a "Hanukkah bush" in Jewish homes. But, in the main, the discussions addressed the concerns of Jewish parents trying to cope with the intrusion of this Christian holiday in their lives and the lives of their children.

All that has changed. No, it is not just that Christmas is, by far, the most important commercial season of the year. And it is not just that virtually every aspect of our culture and society effuses Christmas for nearly two months. Rather, what has changed is the complexion of the Jewish family, due to the astronomical rise in the rate of intermarriage (any marriage between someone born Jewish and someone not born Jewish) and the attendant phenomena of conversionary and mixed-married families. When at least one-fourth of first marriages among born Jews is to a non-Jew (and in some parts of the continent the figure is *one-half*), the indisputable fact is that a majority of Jewish families have within their extended systems members who were not born Jewish and/or are not now Jewish.

All of a sudden, we are not just confronting Christmas in the shopping mall; we must respond to an invitation from a non-Jewish relative to celebrate Christmas with a part of our family. All of a sudden, we are not just debating whether to sing Christmas songs in the school choir; we are asked to accompany a family member to Midnight Mass. It is one thing to say "no" to a child wanting to sit on Santa's knee, but quite another to refuse an invitation from in-laws to celebrate their holiday.

This new situation renders the term "December Dilemma" inadequate, for there is no single dilemma to be faced at this season. Rather, there is a whole series of December Dilemmas—questions, situations, and alternatives that sensitive people must confront when struggling with the issues raised by the proximity of Christmas and H̲anukkah.

—What holiday(s) should I celebrate?
—With whom?
—How?
—When?
—Where?
—What should I do if I do not want to celebrate one holiday or the other?
—Can both holidays be celebrated in one family?
—Is there a difference between "celebrating" a holiday and "observing" a holiday?
—Is there a difference between appreciating another's holiday and appropriating it as one's own?

Obviously, this is a quite complex matter, not easily reduced to a list of simple suggestions. Often, decisions about family celebration of holidays involve far more than religious commitments, however strong or vague. Relationships among family members, promises made or broken, emotional responses that well up unexpectantly—all of these impinge upon the sometimes difficult choices that must be made. And—this point is central—decisions made this year may be up for grabs the next. The evolution of the resolution of our December Dilemmas often takes a long period of time.

It may appear somewhat strange that a book about H̲anukkah is so concerned with Christmas. Yet, we are convinced that, sooner or later, the December Dilemmas emerge in virtually every Jewish family to one degree or another. Our goal is to help you sort out the confusion, point out the problems, and try out some solutions. We will begin by exploring the True Story of Christmas, just as we earlier learned the True (Ever-Evolving) Story of Ḥanukkah. Then, we will turn to the problems surrounding Jews coping with Christmas, converts coping with Christmas, and mixed-marrieds coping with Christmas—each situation has its own subtleties and particular concerns. Finally, we will address the issues raised by religious celebration—both Christian *and* Jewish—in the public domain. Throughout the journey, we will once again hear from our families as they tell how they have dealt with these challenges.

In the end, we hope that you will feel empowered to begin the process of evolving your own answers to the December Dilemmas.

HILKHOT CHRISTMAS

Rabbi Yoḥanan: A non-Jew who studies Torah deserves to die, because...
Torah is our inheritance, not theirs.

Rabbi Meir: A non-Jew who studies the Torah is as holy as the High Priest.

These conflicting opinions are both found in the midst of a Talmudic debate, *Sanhedrin* 49a ff. They express a complete and unresolvable dichotomy, and very clearly represent the diversity of the Jewish experience with non-Jews. Christmas bothers us so much because it is compelling—so is the non-Jew who studies Torah. Christmas threatens us so totally because its basic message is so good—so close to the universalism that Judaism also manifests. We like peace and fellowship. In many ways, Christmas is like the non-Jew studying Torah, a compelling unification of diverse people over common values—and the potential dilution of a uniqueness which gives meaning. Christmas becomes a problem, because it is so close—yet so far away.

As we have said before, one of the most fascinating aspects of our research for this book was the amount of interest Jews have in talking about Christmas. Their reactions to Christmas are a far more interesting topic than their experiences of Ḥanukkah. Drawing and defining the boundaries are more of an issue for most Jews than finding the core meaning in our own celebrations.

If we have learned nothing else, we have found that every North American Jew has his or her own *hilkhot Christmas*, Jewish Laws of how he or she will deal with Christmas. These include such classic examples as "mouthing certain words in the carols," "visiting but not celebrating Christmas," "we go to their house for Christmas and they come to our house for Ḥanukkah/Passover." In essence, our families have taught us that Christmas cannot be escaped; ways have to be found to live with it, without fully living it. Christmas is very much like the non-Jew who studies Torah. In fact, it is in essence non-Jews doing very Jewish things—acting as families and expressing universal values. That is why it is so compelling, and that is why boundaries are so important.

The Havurah

Our family has the great pleasure of being members of a havurah, a group of seven families, who gather together throughout the year for study, celebration and social activities. One evening, I asked the group to reminisce about their experiences with Hanukkah and Christmas.

LARRY NEINSTEIN: I was a closet Christmas caroler. I loved Christmas carols. I was in the madrigal group in high school. We always Christmas caroled around the school.

YOUR AUTHOR: Did you feel any conflict about it?

LARRY NEINSTEIN: I never felt conflict. I was very established in my Jewish identity and did not have a problem. I do remember the season coming on and I knew it was December because in school we started singing the Christmas songs. We had a lot of Jewish kids in public school so we were always singing some Hanukkah songs too.

The kids liked them. Christmas songs were really nice. I remember there was a little girl in grammar school whose parents would not let her get up and sing in the school concert. I felt so sorry for that little girl. I mean, to me at that time those songs had no religious meaning whatsoever. My parents even let me play "Silent Night" for the school concert. We were well-secured in our Jewish identity. It was not even an issue. To me it was nothing. When I got much older, the issue of Christmas and Hanukkah changed.

BEVERLY WEISE: I grew up in Chicago in a not very Jewish neighborhood. I remember feeling that if I sang "Silent Night" that I was absolutely giving up my Jewish identity. I felt it was a major sin and I felt like I betrayed the Jewish people.

I think my parents said it was okay if I mouthed the words and God would know I didn't mean it.

TOBI INLANDER: I grew up in a real un-Jewish community. I was one of two Jews in any classroom. I was always the one who was asked or volunteered to come in when they were doing "This is what Christmas means and this is what Hanukkah means."

The first time I felt conflict was when I was older and I got my first job at fifteen and a half. I was working in a store and people were wearing Christmas Bells and I had to decide whether I should wear Christmas Bells. Would it mean anything if I wore those little bells while I was working in the store?

YOUR AUTHOR: What did you do?

TOBI INLANDER: I wore them.

YOUR AUTHOR: Did you feel uncomfortable with them?

TOBI INLANDER: I guess I did a little bit, but it didn't feel like a religious thing to me. It was more about being in a good mood with everybody else. Of course, I did not show up at my grandmother's house with the bells on.

BEVERLY WEISE: I remember once driving to Palm Springs with the Shapiros and we were all singing Christmas carols. Rabbi Shapiro knew every word, syllable and refrain. He knew them all by heart. He grew up in the Midwest and he loves them.

I remember when I was seven or so seeing some famous Jewish comedian on Ed Sullivan who invented the term "Hanukkah bush" in 1958. It must have been Jackie Mason, probably.

So my girlfriend and I said "Let's buy a Hanukkah bush." They were selling little Christmas trees about twelve inches tall for a dollar. So between the two of us, we rounded up a dollar and bought the tree.

I'll never forget it. We were *so* scared walking home with that tree. It was like a major thing. We were so afraid of getting caught. There was this Orthodox rabbi who lived across the street and we thought he would see us and tell my parents. But, we decided we were going to do this. We ran through the alleys to get to my friend's home. My mother happened to be talking on the phone to my friend's Mom. We walk in and her Mom said "What have you got there?" We say, "A Hanukkah bush. We are going to decorate it with little Hanukkah objects." Well, I heard my mother scream at the other end. I mean, don't ask. The bottom line was that there was no way that they were going to have that.

YOUR AUTHOR: So, what did they do?

BEVERLY WEISE:	Actually, something quite brilliant. They decided to let us decorate the tree and then donate it to a hospital. And that is what we did.
IRA GOODBERG:	Like it or not, Christmas has become a national holiday. We are living in a Christian nation. There is no getting around it. You can say the theory of the constitution is that church and state are separated, but the United States of America is a Protestant country. It always has been.
BONNIE GOODBERG:	But, Christmas is a religious holiday.
IRA GOODBERG:	It's lost its religiosity. Christmas was greatly confused by the misuse of a guy sliding down a chimney and if you were lucky enough to be a kid you got presents. That did not relate to Christianity.
BEVERLY WEISE:	That is what my aunt used to say. She would say that if the Christians were more Christian, it would not be a problem.

The Bobrow Family

The Bobrow Family has faced all the complications of the winter holidays arising from a conversionary marriage. Their honest and direct conversation reveals a sensitivity and sense of humor that defuses what could be a terribly tense situation.

YOUR AUTHOR:	What do you think of Hanukkah in terms of other holidays?
ALISSA:	It is one of the least.
YOUR AUTHOR:	What do you mean by the least?
ALISSA:	It is one of the least important when you have Yom Kippur, Rosh Ha-Shana and you have Shabbats and because most of the most important holidays are in the Bible. Hanukkah is not in the Bible. It is in the Book of Maccabees which is not part of the Bible.
YOUR AUTHOR:	Are you looking forward to Hanukkah?

ALISSA: I am looking forward to it, but I don't think it is a very important holiday. It is important because we got our freedom but otherwise it is not. But, I get presents.

YOUR AUTHOR: Is there another Jewish holiday that you think is more fun or more important for you?

ALISSA: I like Pesa<u>h</u> because I like to sit at the table and sing Passover songs and eat all of the food. I like that holiday.

YOUR AUTHOR: Do you like Christmas trees?

DAVID: Yeah, they are pretty. They are very nice but I don't think they really mean anything. There is no purpose in a Christmas tree. It is something to look nice in your house. Maybe there is a purpose to the Christians. It says something to them. All of the symbols have to do with winter and making them Christian, like snow. If you see snow, oh, you think of Christmas. You see a pine tree, you think of Christmas and all that stuff. Even stars they make, they say it's the Christmas star or whatever.

YOUR AUTHOR: You see Christmas in your grandmother's house. How does that feel to you?

DAVID: It doesn't bug me or anything. It is something I have gotten used to. I don't look at it as a religious experience or anything. I just am going to my grandma's house or to my aunt's and uncle's house, you know, to be with them. I don't think of it as being there for Christmas. We are usually there when it is during <u>H</u>anukkah, not every year. Sometimes <u>H</u>anukkah can be two weeks before Christmas and they give us <u>H</u>anukkah presents then, not Christmas presents.

YOUR AUTHOR: When you go over there, do you think that is an important holiday for them?

CLAUDIA: Well, I don't think that my family is very religious and very observant. I think it is something that they do because it is something everybody does. Everybody does Christmas and they have always done it. It is a tradition.

YOUR AUTHOR: Shlomo, how did you handle all of Claudia's struggles with her family?

SHLOMO: I felt that I should stay aside and let her work it out herself. I did not want her to feel that I was putting pressure on her to do certain things. I felt that if I really put pressure on her, it might backfire. She might resent it. I had confidence in her Jewishness that she would do the right thing. The only thing I said was "no Christmas tree." A Christmas tree was out.

YOUR AUTHOR: When did you say that?

CLAUDIA: Before we even got married. We met during Hanukkah to begin with or very shortly thereafter, so the issue came up immediately when we met. I wanted to convert even before we met. Shlomo would say "You realize that you cannot have a Christmas tree if you are Jewish." That was a real hard thing to give up, but I knew that he was right. It just seemed rather obvious. So that is how we worked it out. I know other couples where the Jewish partner wavers on that issue which I think is a mistake.

YOUR AUTHOR: If you were so strong about not having a Christmas tree in the house, why did you decide to go along with Claudia's solution to visit her parents on Christmas? Wasn't that a strange thing for you to do?

SHLOMO: We struggled with it for a few years, we were skipping town and so forth and so on and we were afraid of the influence on the kids. I think after we discussed it back and forth, we came to the conclusion together that trying to avoid it is sometimes worse than confronting it. I thought this is the best solution for the situation. I think we felt confident in the education that we gave our kids. They have a pretty strong Jewish background and I am not afraid of them being influenced.

CLAUDIA: The first couple of years we were married, all we celebrated were the High Holidays and Hanukkah. We did not do anything for the other holidays. After the kids came, we started thinking in terms of their education and decided that they would go to a Jewish Day School. Then, we started looking into some of the Jewish things. It did not happen overnight. Gradually, we realized that if we were more involved with the entire Jewish year, by the time we would get to Christmas, it would not be such a problem.

At first, I did not know about Sukkot. Then later on we were invited to someone's house for Sukkot and they had this nice thing in the backyard. After that, I started bugging Shlomo to build one. He said, "You don't want to do that. Nobody does that here, only the religious people." So finally I bugged him enough years and finally he said we would do it. So, we put up a little *sukkah* in the backyard and I remember coming in and saying, "Shlomo, I am going to decorate the living daylights out of this thing. I am getting all of my Christmas frustrations out on this *sukkah*. This is terrific. I am making little decorations. By the time Christmas comes, I won't have a problem." I was right. When Christmas came, I did not have a problem because I had put all of that energy into the Jewish holiday. Then I realized that is what you have to do. You have to celebrate all of the holidays the rest of the year. Then when you get to Hanukkah, you really don't have a big conflict. If your life is filled with Jewish festivals and a Jewish calendar is part of your life, by the time you get to Christmas, it's no problem.

YOUR AUTHOR: So why do you go to your parents for Christmas? Is it for you or is it for your parents?

CLAUDIA: No, it is for them. It is for them. Last year we decided that they could celebrate our Hanukkah with us. It is only fair that if we go to them for Christmas, they should come to us for Hanukkah. We are not going to church with them. I would draw the line when it comes to that. I don't see a point in doing it. We are going over there to get together with the family. And, you have to remember they are coming to me for Sukkot. They are coming to me for Pesah. They come to me on *Shabbes*. My mother doesn't do anything for Easter. We don't go there for Easter. The only holidays she celebrates are Thanksgiving and Christmas and on Thanksgiving they usually come here. It is the least you can do.

The Gindis

The experience of the winter holidays in America is a long way from Aleppo, Syria, for Jack and Rae Gindi. Yet, as their family took root in the New World, they found themselves confronted with all the dilemmas of December.

YOUR AUTHOR:	What was your experience with Christmas as a kid?
JACK:	None at all.
YOUR AUTHOR:	Your mother never took you to see Santa Claus?
JACK:	No.
YOUR AUTHOR:	You never sat on Santa's lap?
RAE:	I did. My mother used to take us to visit Santa Claus every year. Santa Claus was not a religious experience for me. It was a fun experience. Our background was strong enough where our Judaism was never threatened by anything from the outside. We could enjoy what was going on out there without a feeling that it would compromise our religion.

The Coblens

Elke Coblens shared two experiences of Christmas Day.

ELKE:	We've done lots of things on Christmas Day. Sometimes, we go to Palm Springs. This year, Erev Christmas is when we had the *havurah* Hanukkah party. We figured, what else are Jewish people going to do on *Erev* Christmas? We will have our Hanukkah party, then everybody has something to do.
	One year, we were in Palm Springs on Christmas Eve and we wanted to get something to eat. Well, everything was closed, except Fromins Deli, but there was an hour and a half wait. We found a Circle K market and they had a microwave. We took out a pizza, heated it up, and ate it in the car. Rosa said it was okay to eat there because "Circle K" meant it was kosher like "Ⓤ."

The Kirsch Family

The Kirsch family has engaged in many of the battles surrounding the place of Christmas and Hanukkah in the public schools. And, they are finding it a difficult political and emotional struggle.

JENNIFER: I think I am lucky because I have a Jewish teacher. With other teachers, they are usually Christian and you only learn about Christmas. But since I have a Jewish teacher, we learned about Hanukkah and we had a party with Christmas cookies and Hanukkah cookies. We had a mother come in and tell us about the menorahs and Hanukkah.

YOUR AUTHOR: What did you learn about Christmas?

JENNIFER: Well, last year I did a report on Christmas in other countries. Mine was on Ireland and what I learned was that they leave two wooden shoes and carrots and sugar and milk and cookies for Santa, because in Ireland Santa does not come on a reindeer; he comes on a horse.

ANN: I have noticed a big difference in the militancy of the Jewish parents in the public elementary schools. In years past, certainly when we were kids, you sang Christmas songs. If they included "I Had a Little Dreidle," you considered yourself lucky. In the last couple of years, especially this year, there have been more parents that have been unwilling to have Christmas taught and it has created a lot of controversy. In Jennifer's elementary school, there were even some silly things like, if there was going to be a Christmas tree in the school, it had to have a dreidle on it.

ADAM: I never learned about Christmas in school, except we sang some songs, but not really religious ones. Dad, why don't you mind me singing about Christmas?

JONATHAN: I don't mind it because you know who you are and I know that you know what your religion is and what we value because you are a good student and you participate in all of the holidays and you go to Hebrew School. That is why I don't worry.

ADAM: Okay.

ANN: When the kids were little, like three or four, they began to get the idea that there was a major holiday that was celebrated a certain way and theirs was left out. I remember once Adam asked me why there were no Hanukkah displays in the May Company department store and I said "I don't know. Why don't we find out?" So, Adam went up to this saleslady and asked her. She couldn't answer, but she was rather sympathetic.

ADAM: We have some close friends who live a block away. They are Christian and we go to their house usually every Christmas and I help decorate their Christmas tree and we have a party with them. We recognize that it is just a way of helping them celebrate. I don't think there is anything wrong with helping them sing Christmas carols or trimming their tree. We go to their house on Christmas Eve and give them a Christmas present and they come to our house on Hanukkah and they bring us Hanukkah presents. They come to our Seders and to our *sukkah*, too.

The issues surrounding the December Dilemmas are so complex that we interviewed two additional families who have faced the situations that arise when there are Christian members of the family.

Carol and Eric Mills

Carol and Eric Mills have been married for ten years. Eric converted to Judaism on their first anniversary, having grown up in what he describes as a "non-religious" Episcopalian family. He and Carol decided to withdraw from Christmas when their children Ian, 7, and Seth, 4, arrived on the scene. Although the Millses belong to a Conservative synagogue and send the boys to religious school, the threat of Christmas confusing their children was too real to ignore.

ERIC: We talked about how we would handle the holiday problem as soon as we seriously considered marriage. The first year we were married, we went to my parents for Christmas and there they had our presents wrapped in Christmas paper. It just didn't feel comfortable.

CAROL: We knew that if we felt uncomfortable as adults, it would be very hard for our kids to sort out the holidays and their feelings about it. So, eventually, we told Eric's parents that we would not be coming to them for Christmas.

The first ground rule we established was that we wanted our kids to get H̲anukkah gifts from Eric's parents, wrapped as H̲anukkah gifts, on H̲anukkah.

YOUR AUTHOR: How did they feel about that?

ERIC: It was difficult for them to understand what our objections were to Christmas. For them, Christmas is not a religious thing. It's more about gifts and the good feelings of the season. I'm not even sure they go to church.

CAROL: Yes they do. Your Mom and brother go every year.

ERIC: We just thought it was something we wanted our kids to not have to deal with.

CAROL: It's so tough to see all the hoopla around Christmas and not want to be part of it. I remember wanting Christmas as a child, even though I knew it wasn't mine and I couldn't have it. My mother distanced us from Christmas to make it easier on us. Now that I am doing the same, I can appreciate how helpful it is.

ERIC: We felt it would be difficult to explain that "this is what Grandma and Grandpa do, but we don't do it at our house."

CAROL: Eric's family is very close, so this was a tough thing for them to accept.

ERIC: They've grown with it. Originally, my Mom was very hurt. She didn't understand why we couldn't participate. But, she has a hard time understanding why we don't do Halloween or Valentine's Day either. She kept insisting: "Christmas is not a religious thing." But, it is a religious thing.

CAROL: The other problem was your Christmas stocking.

ERIC: You see, until ten years ago, I was there with my family for Christmas. Now, I am not. Each member of my family has a stocking with his or her name on it. It was really hard for my Mom when I asked her to take my stocking down. It's emotionally hard for her. But, to her everlasting credit, she has done everything we have asked.

CAROL: I am sure that each year there are hurt feelings. We just can't be one family on that day. But, we do recognize their holiday. We go shopping for presents and have them wrapped in Christmas paper. We take the presents to their house and place them under the tree. We just are not there on Christmas morning when the gifts are opened.

ERIC: I will go have Christmas dinner later that day with my family. Every year it's pot roast, and peas—you know, the traditional Christmas dinner in our house. I don't take Carol or the kids with me. It's a way for me to stay a part of the family and share their holiday with them.

CAROL: We celebrate with Eric's family a lot through the year. Birthdays are a big thing, every other year we go to them for Thanksgiving, and there are other celebrations.

I have never regretted the decision. Our kids feel strongly Jewish. We make Hanukkah as wonderful as possible, along with the other Jewish holidays. They have never really asked us if they could go for Christmas. They truly know it's not their holiday.

As we shall see, one of the dilemmas of conversionary or mixed-married families is what to do about invitations for Christmas from Christian members of the extended family. We wondered how a Jewish parent whose adult child has married someone not born Jewish feels when the decision is to spend Christmas with the Christian in-laws.

Lila and Sheldon Schein

We asked Lila and Sheldon Schein, parents of Linda and Lorin Fife, whose family was interviewed for The Art of Jewish Living: The Passover Seder, *how they feel about this issue.*

SHEL: When Linda first married Lorin, we were very concerned about the kids. We asked them to raise the kids Jewish and they assured us they would.

LILA: They did not go to Lorin's parents for Christmas when the kids were little. They brought up the children in a wonderfully warm and observant Jewish environment. In fact, they are much more observant than we ever were.

SHEL: Now that the kids are older, I think they do take the kids to the *"machetonim"* (the in-laws) for Christmas, but it's not a big deal.

LILA: I have absolutely no concern about the grandchildren going to a Christmas celebration. They have their Jewish identities so firmly imprinted on their minds that Christmas would have no significance for them whatsoever. If they didn't have such a strong Jewish feeling, I'd feel threatened.

YOUR AUTHOR: Have you ever been invited to Lorins' parents home for Christmas?

SHEL: No, I think they know that it would put us in a difficult spot.

YOUR AUTHOR: It seems like this is working out for you. If it hadn't, if the grandchildren were not getting a good Jewish education and they were celebrating Christmas, would you say something? Do you think it's your role to say something?

LILA: Look. Every parent has a different attitude about this. Some of my friends are in a situation like you describe, but they would never say a word. Me, I'm not afraid to open my mouth. Sure, I'd let my kids know how I feel. It's much easier for grandchildren to turn towards the Gentile world. We'd lose them. Of course, it would be their decision. I'd have to go along with whatever they'd decide. But, I'd be crushed.

THE TRUE STORY OF CHRISTMAS

Christmas is one of the most important holidays in Christianity. The religious significance of the celebration can be learned from the word "Christmas" which means "the Mass of Christ," Mass being the term for the traditional worship service of the Catholic church, which was the *only* Christian church for many centuries. The term "Christ" means "Messiah," and therein lies the fundamental problem of Christmas for Jews. Christians believe that the man called Jesus of Nazareth was the son of God, the Messiah; Jews do not. Christmas celebrates the birthday of Jesus *Christ*.

Although the Christian Bible records the birth of Jesus in the Gospels of Luke (2:1-19) and Matthew (2:1-23), there is no certainty that December 25 was the actual date. In fact, the first historical indication that an observance was held to mark the day came in the year 336 C.E. in the *Philocalian Calendarm*, a Roman almanac. Fourteen years later, December 25 was officially adopted as the date of Christmas in the Roman Catholic church by Pope Julius I. (But, some of the Eastern Orthodox churches to this day celebrate Christmas on January 6.)The Emperor Justinian made Christmas a civic holiday in the year 529 C.E., fully 500 years after the time of Jesus.

This date was probably chosen in response to the existence of pagan midwinter celebrations. Winter was a fearful time for ancient peoples. The days were short, plunging the people in darkness for most of their waking hours. The sun, a revered deity of the pagans, lost much of its power. The people would use greens, a reminder of spring, and lights, a symbol of joy, to help brighten the dark days and nights.

Most students of Christian ritual acknowledge that the origin of what came to be the Christmas tree probably began with these pagans who would bring an evergreen tree indoors during the winter season. The tree was so closely associated with the pagans that early church celebrations banned its use for Christmas! But, as with many popular rituals, the people continued the practice. And so the church had to do what the Rabbis often did—infuse a pagan custom with new religious meaning and significance.

So how did the church fathers reinterpret the Christmas tree? First, it is an evergreen, representing the eternal life of the Christ. Its shape is ascending, towards heaven, where the resurrected Jesus arose. The star on the top is the Star of Bethlehem, birthplace of the Christ child. The sap of the tree is the blood of Christ.

Although there are historical mentions of Christmas trees dating from the Middle Ages, it was not until the 1930's that North Americans made the tree an integral part of the Christmas celebration. Today, the National Christmas Tree Association estimates that 30 million natural trees are cut down and sold for Christmas *every year*.

The roots of mistletoe and holly can also be traced back to the pagans. The ancient Druids believed that holly guarded against witches, thunder and lightning. At the winter solstice, they cut mistletoe during an elaborate ceremony in the forest that included sacrifices to their gods. Priests then divided the mistletoe among the people, who hung it in their homes as an amulet against evil.

Kissing under the mistletoe came about because of an ancient Scandinavian myth involving a God slain by a dart made from mistletoe. From then on, it was determined that mistletoe should never again be responsible for anyone's death, so it was declared a sign of love, not hate. When brought into the home at Christmas time, the custom evolved that those who pass under the mistletoe should kiss.

Holly was used by Christians to make wreaths to symbolize the crown of thorns Jesus wore to his death. Legend has it that this crown was plaited with holly berries that were white before the crucifixion and red afterward.

Candles, originally used to light up the dark nights of winter, are symbols of Jesus, "the light unto the world." Placing a single candle in the window at Christmas was an Irish custom. It is said that Catholics in Ireland would put a candle in the window during religious persecutions to indicate to fugitive priests that they were welcome inside the home to say Mass. The lights of the Christmas tree and the decorative lights on homes comes from this tradition.

The creche (crib)—a nativity scene depicting the birth of Jesus as told in the Gospels—is traced to Saint Francis of Assisi in the year 1223 C.E.

And, last, but certainly not least, Santa Claus. He is not just some jolly old fat man who has a stable of elves and reindeer somewhere north of Alaska. That is a very late 19th and 20th century version of the character. In fact, Santa is a fantasy figure derived from a Catholic bishop by the name of Saint Nicholas, born in the third century C.E., who was famous for giving unexpected gifts. He became the patron saint of children, who brought them gifts upon his visits, much as the three Wise Men who visited the manger brought presents to the newborn Jesus in Bethlehem. Scandinavian tradition links Santa with Thor, the god of fire—thus, the red-faced chimney sweep.

"But," you protest, "nobody believes in this religious stuff anymore. Most of my Christian neighbors probably don't know about these things."

Ah, but that is not the point. For even if one were to ignore all the religious symbolism of these objects, they have most certainly come to be associated with Christmas. The tree, the mistletoe, the holly—even the eggnog—are all recognized as symbols of Christmas, a Christian holiday.

Or, is it?

This question brings us to the heart of the argument—is Christmas a religious or a secular holiday? After all, Christmas is a legal holiday on the calendar. Virtually everything is closed on Christmas, including governmental offices. Public schools close for days surrounding the holiday. And, as we will see below, no less than the United States Supreme Court has decided that the Christmas tree is a secular, not a religious, symbol.

Ironically, when it comes to Christmas, religious Jews and religious Christians face the same problem: how to put the "Christ" back into Christmas. Once Christmas is secularized, its religious meanings reduced to insignificance, it becomes that much easier for the "unchurched" to see in the tree and its holiday only warm family times, gifts from Santa, and chestnuts roasting on an open fire.

WHO'S CELEBRATING?

With the secularization of Christmas, it has become more common to find Jews who celebrate some aspects of the holiday. The most recent surveys indicate that 10% of born Jews report having Christmas trees in their homes, 25% of Jews-by-Choice have Christmas trees, and 70-80% of mixed-marrieds erect a tree for Christmas.

But, trees and trimming are only half the story. In its pervasiveness, the Christmas holiday presents a challenge to born Jews, converts, and mixed-marrieds that forces decisions to be made and boundary lines drawn.

Jews who celebrate Christmas are embracing symbols and traditions that are absolutely foreign to Judaism. There is no connection between Hanukkah and Christmas except that because of the vagaries of the calendar, they come together at the same time of year. Christmas is the celebration of the birth of a Messiah in whom the Jews do not believe, while Hanukkah is the celebration of the right not to assimilate—which is the very thing that Jews who celebrate Christmas are doing.

The question is: Why do Jews in America bring these non-Jewish customs into their homes and their lives? One reason is clearly a lack of knowledge about what Christmas means. Or, some believe that the Christmas rituals have been so stripped of their spiritual meaning that the tree, the egg nog, and Santa are more secular than religious, and therefore relatively benign. Others have given in to the pressures exerted by the mass media, peers, the work place, and even family members.

For some, the adoption of Christmas customs stems from the demands of their young children. Try to remember how overwhelmingly enticing the Christmas season is—even to young Jewish girls and boys. Santa Claus, elves, candy canes, presents under beautifully decorated trees, brightly colored lights adorning houses in the neighborhood—these are powerful attractions to any child.

So, when the family takes its stroll through the mall and happens upon Santa's North Pole, and a wide-eyed three-year-old asks "Can I sit on Santa's knee?," the parent is presented with one of the challenges of the Christmas season, a December Dilemma.

The Jewish parent's answer to the child will depend on several things: the intensity of the parent's Jewish commitments, the parent's assessment of how "influential" the visit on Santa's knee might be on the child's Jewish identity, and, perhaps most importantly, the parent's ability to set limits.

On the one hand, no one wants her/his child to feel deprived of anything, especially, if what the child wants seems on the surface so harmless. Isn't Santa just some sort of "man in a costume," like Mickey Mouse at Disneyland? Moreover, there is a deep-seated wish in many Jews to be accepted, to be part of the majority, to be equal in the eyes of society. If we deny our children Santa, will they feel left out, inferior, different, frustrated, envious? Will they want him even more?

On the other hand, many parents simply hate to say "no" to their children. We want them to have everything. Yet, there are certainly lots of things our children ask us for to which we do say "no." Not for some capricious use of parental authority, but because we value their health, their safety, and their well-being. So, we occasionally say "no" to more candy, or running across the street, or watching violent television shows. We say "no" when we believe we have the responsibility as parents to teach them, to guide them, to help mold their character and sense of identity.

And thus, many Jewish parents say "no" to Santa Claus and Christmas trees because they are not part of being Jewish and we are Jewish. You, my child, are Jewish. Christmas is not our holiday. But, "just say no" doesn't seem to be enough of an answer. And this leads us to one powerful explanation of why Hanukkah has been elevated to the status of one of the most observed Jewish holidays.

Christmas is not our holiday. "Hanukkah is our holiday," the parent will rush to add. So, the first instinct is to offer an alternative to Christmas. Many parents are thankful that there is one. Yet, even more important may be to seize this seemingly negative episode and turn it into a lesson in Jewish identity building and child development.

Early childhood educators tell us that one of the most crucial stages in socialization occurs when a child is between 18 and 30 months old and attends another child's birthday party. When the birthday cake is brought in, most of the little guests try to blow out the candles right along with the birthday child. As the child opens presents, little hands start to grab for the toys. Why do you think "party favors" were invented? To help children begin to distinguish between what's mine and what's his/hers. Toddlers must learn the difference between celebrating one's own birthday and celebrating another's.

Thus, many Jewish educators will advise parents to give their children who want to celebrate Christmas a very important message: Christmas is someone else's party, not ours. Just as we can appreciate someone else's birthday celebration and be happy for them, we can wonder at how beautiful Christmas is, but it is not our party.

And then, many parents make a perfectly understandable, but incomplete leap. "Christmas is for Christians. They have Christmas. We are Jewish. We have Hanukkah." In an attempt to substitute something for Christmas, the parent offers Hanukkah. In fact, Hanukkah is even better than Christmas. "Christmas is only one day. Hanukkah is for eight!" So, now, as incredible as it seems, the parental anxiety leads to the teaching that our party lasts longer, offers more presents, and is just as beautiful.

Of course, the problem is that it just isn't true. Hanukkah cannot hold a candle to Christmas. As we have learned, it is a minor event in the Jewish holiday cycle and has never, until recently, been viewed as a central celebration for the Jewish people. Therefore, the customs and ceremonies surrounding Hanukkah pale by comparison to those of Christmas—which is one of the two major holidays of Christianity.

In fact, it seems clear that among Jews who stand on the periphery of Jewish life, the attempt to combat Christmas with Hanukkah is doomed to failure. Even the sometimes outrageous attempts by mass marketers to inflate the importance of Hanukkah as the "Jewish alternative" to Christmas feel wrong in some fundamental way. "Hanukkah Harry" and "Hanukkah bushes" and even "Smiley Shalom," a Jewish version of "Frosty the Snowman," cannot hope to compete with the magnificence of the Christmas celebration.

The answer to the child is incomplete. "We're Jewish—we have Hanukkah" is only the beginning of the response. "We're Jewish, and we have—Hanukkah, Sukkot, Passover, Shavuot, Purim, Simḥat Torah, Rosh Ha-Shanah, Yom Kippur, Lag B'Omer, Yom ha-Atzma'ut, Tu B'Shvat—and, most importantly, Shabbat every week." The child who has experienced the building of a *Sukkah* will not feel deprived of trimming a tree. The child who has participated in a meaningful Passover Seder will not feel deprived of Christmas dinner. The child who has paraded with the Torah on Simḥat Torah, planted trees at Tu B'Shvat, brought first fruits at Shavuot, given *mishloaḥ manot* at Purim, and welcomed the Shabbat weekly with candles and wine and *ḥallah* by the time s/he is three years old will understand that to be Jewish is to be enriched by a calendar brimming with joyous celebration.

Then, of course, there are parents who believe the December lesson that Jews are different than almost everybody else is an inescapable part of being Jewish, unless you live in Israel. There is a great value in being unique, different, valuable in your own right. In fact, for them, the celebration of Hanukkah in proximity to Christmas is a boon. They want their children to identify with the Maccabees' struggle for religious liberty and for the right *not* to assimilate into the majority culture. Is this not the very same struggle that we Jews living in a predominantly Christian society must also wage?

At the same time, most Jews are comfortable in the North American society. The great promise of religious freedom has indeed created the diversity of culture that characterizes the free world. When we live side-by-side with other religious peoples, we must respect and appreciate their customs, arts and traditions.

What does appreciation mean? It means that there is nothing wrong with enjoying the beauty of someone else's celebration. Is there any doubt that the music of Christmas is lovely and quite moving? Any number of rabbis and educators will admit that they are "closet carolers." How can one grow up in this culture and not learn the words to the song "White Christmas?" Can we deny the beauty of the Christmas tree, its ornaments and decorations? Not really. Shall we be embarrassed at finding ourselves moved to tears by the Christmas scene in the film "It's a Wonderful Life?" If we are strong in our Jewish commitments, there is little danger that appreciating the warmth and beauty of another's holiday will threaten our fundamental identity.

But appreciation does not mean appropriation. Because appropriation leads to confusion, loss of identity and, ultimately, assimilation. And assimilation is what the Maccabees and generations of Jews after them fought so hard to prevent. To appropriate Christmas into our homes would give posthumous victory to Antiochus. Christmas does not belong in a Jewish home—period.

RELIGIOUS HOLIDAYS IN THE PUBLIC DOMAIN

One of the terribly difficult problems for Jews during December is the celebration of Christmas as an official "legal" holiday. Offices, banks, and virtually every retail establishment is closed on Christmas Day. Public schools close, not just for the day, but for a two-week "Christmas Vacation" surrounding the holiday. And, in many cities and towns across North America, government property features holiday displays, ranging from Christmas trees to Nativity scenes.

For Jewish children who attend public schools, the introduction of Christmas into the curriculum during the weeks preceding the holiday throws them and their parents into a yearly confrontation with their minority status. More than one Jewish parent has marched into a principal's office when their child brought home a Christmas art project or tree ornament, or debated the singing of Christmas carols in the annual winter concert, or agonized over a child's taking a role in the Christmas pageant.

Most Jewish organizations with interests in this area—community relations councils, the American Jewish Committee, the Anti-Defamation League—have strongly pressed the case for the separation of church and state as reason enough for the elimination of religious holiday celebrations in the public schools. They point out that Christmas is an important Christian holy day that not all students celebrate. They argue that Christmas plays which portray religious themes have no place in public schools. They maintain that neither Christmas nor Hanukkah should be celebrated in this setting.

Yet, most officials of the Jewish community realize that it is difficult, if not impossible, to police thousands of teachers throughout the land to prevent these celebrations. Much work is done to sensitize school personnel to the feelings of Jewish children at this time of year. Alternative celebration suggestions are made: produce a "winter festival" that preserves the holiday atmosphere, but removes the religious connotations. Study about different religious celebrations around the world at this time of year. Use the holiday season as an opportunity to celebrate the unity of humankind.

Some Jewish groups have distributed brochures which state the position of the community. Here is an example from a booklet entitled "December Dilemma," published by the Jewish Community Council of Detroit, Michigan:

WHAT IS APPROPRIATE?

The following are examples of activities which are appropriate (during the holiday season):

1. Education about the principles of religious freedom and religious liberty
2. Intercultural programs which focus on the role religion has played in the development of society
3. Factual and objective teaching about religion
4. Religious symbols used by individual students as a model of self-expression

5.   The study of religious music as part of a music appreciation course, or as part of a study of various lands and cultures

6.   Recognition of a student's absence from school due to a religious holiday as an excused absence

WHAT IS NOT APPROPRIATE?

1.   Organized prayer
2.   Distribution of Bibles
3.   The public display or presentation of religious symbols by school authorities
4.   Presentation of religious plays and films in a religious context
5.   Religious programs or prayer meetings during the school day
6.   Penalizing students for an absence due to a religious holiday
7.   Singing of Christmas carols and/or Hanukkah songs.

Another arena of conflict is the public display of religious symbols on government property. For years, Christmas trees and Nativity scenes figured prominently in holiday displays at city halls, county courthouses, and public parks. Most Jewish leaders joined groups such as the American Civil Liberties Union to argue in the public press and even in court that these religious symbols violate the separation of church and state. Some Jewish groups, one in particular, took another tack and fought for the inclusion of Hanukkah symbols in the holiday decorations.

A key argument in the debate surrounds the definition of what constitutes a "religious" symbol. In a landmark decision reached in 1988, the United States Supreme Court ruled that Christmas trees are not religious symbols and may therefore be placed on government property. The court also ruled that Hanukkah menorahs are also not religious objects. Nativity scenes were ruled "religious" and discouraged by the court.

This decision, of course, did nothing to help those who argue against Christmas trees on government property. But, it did open the door for fundamentalist Jewish groups to place Hanukkah menorahs right next to the Christmas tree in the lobbies of city halls across the land.

Even so, some communities have continued to oppose the intrusion of Hanukkah onto the Christmas scene. In a remarkable story that unfolded in Westlake Village, California, a suburb of Los Angeles, the dilemma facing the Jewish community is revealed in all its glory:

LOS ANGELES TIMES

DECEMBER 21, 1989

WESTLAKE VILLAGE BANS

MENORAH IN CITY HALL

BY LESLIE BERGER

TIMES STAFF WRITER

A Jewish center's request to display a Hanukkah menorah next to the Westlake Village City Hall Christmas tree has been denied by officials who said the eight-day celebration is not a national holiday and that it lacks the secular appeal of Christmas.

City manager Larry Bagley, who rejected a request made earlier this month to display the menorah, also said the City Hall reception area was too small to accommodate decorations for cultural holidays not endorsed by the state or federal government.

The decision has ignited fears of anti-Semitism among Jews and prompted dozens of concerned telephone calls to Chabad of the Conejo, a community group with synagogues and cultural centers in Westlake Village and Agoura Hills, associate director Rabbi Yitzchak Sapochkinsky said Wednesday.

Sapochkinsky said he did not think the city's motives were anti-Semitic, although he called the decision by Bagley "a shameful thing."

Bagley said he knew of the U.S. Supreme Court decision last July that a menorah, like a Christmas tree, is a secular symbol and therefore could be publicly displayed without violating constitutional bans on governmental endorsement of religions. But Bagley said the decision simply allowed—but did not require—that menorahs be displayed.

"I wouldn't want anybody of any particular cultural group to feel we weren't concerned or didn't have good thoughts for their religious or cultural symbols," Bagley said.

Sapochkinsky estimated that several thousand Jews live in the Conejo Valley, mostly in Thousand Oaks and Agoura Hills. Both of those cities approved Chabad requests to display a menorah, and the Thousand Oaks City Council last week held a menorah-lighting ceremony at the start of its regular meeting.

Westlake Village Mayor Bonnie Klove said the council would not reconsider Bagley's decision before the start of the eight-day Hanukkah celebration tomorrow night. She said that while a Christmas tree is a secular symbol, a menorah is a religious symbol.

Mayor Pro Tem Ken Rufener agreed in a December 11 letter to Rabbi Moshe Bryski, Chabad's regional director. "Christmas is a festive season shared by people of all religions and backgrounds," Rufener wrote. "Surely you are aware that Jewish families in our community, as well as Christian families, give and attend Christmas parties."

CONFUSION IN THE MARKETPLACE

One of the more interesting of the December Dilemmas is the confusion between Christmas and Hanukkah in the marketplace. In their rush to commercialize the winter holidays, entrepreneurs regularly confuse the meanings of Hanukkah and Christmas. We see evergreen trees sold to Jews as "Hanukkah bushes;" blue and white lights to decorate the home inside and out; "Hanukkah Harry," an ersatz Jewish Santa Claus who visits little Jewish boys and girls with Hanukkah presents; "Hannuklaus," a mixed image of Santa Claus, a dreidle and a Star of David; greeting cards with Santa lighting a menorah; holiday displays of blue and white tinsel surrounding a *hanukkiyah*; Hanukkah stockings in blue and white, embroidered with dreidles, Star of David designs and the word "Shalom."

There are stories of Hanukkah-Christmas confusion that are both mysterious and downright offensive. Take the case of the chocolate Maccabees that one of the large Jewish candymakers imported for Hanukkah one year. Although wrapped in foil imprinted with images of bearded Maccabees, somehow the chocolate itself changed from Maccabees to Santa Clauses en route from Israel!

Then, there is the more recent case of "mouse-taken" identity fostered by no less than Steven Spielberg and McDonald's restaurants. The animated film "An American Tail" was cause for cheer in the Jewish community when it appeared as a holiday offering in the winter of 1986. Finally, Jewish parents could take their children to a film featuring a Jewish hero, a mouse-child by the name of Fievel Mousekowitz, who immigrates with his family from Russia to America at the turn of the 20th century. There is no question of Fievel's heritage; the film features a Hanukkah celebration in his home in Russia.

So, you can imagine the consternation of thousands of Jewish parents who found Fievel the Jewish mouse featured on a Christmas stocking promotional tie-in in McDonald's restaurants within days of the film's debut! Almost immediately, a Jewish educator from Seattle, Washington, Patti Moskovitz (no relation to Fievel!), began a campaign to have the stocking retracted by the Spielberg and McDonald's people. Although assured by the promoters that "millions of dollars" were at stake, and that there was no chance that the promotion would be cancelled, Patti and dozens of other concerned Jewish parents, educators, and communal officials put enough pressure on those concerned to force the mixed-message mistake off the market.

Some children's literature has also appeared that is quite disturbing. A few years ago, a book featuring a "Bubbie and Zadie" who live in Alaska and answer the wish lists of good Jewish boys and girls appeared.

On the other hand, it has become increasingly clear, year after year, that the merchants and mass media mavens have finally discovered Hanukkah. Not long ago, it would have been unthinkable to see Hanukkah decorations in store windows, "Happy Hanukkah" greetings on television, or inclusive "Season's Greetings" messages on fast-food packaging. Today, they are the norm.

Some of the changes are subtle. "Christmas Gift Ideas" have become "Holiday Gift Ideas." "Christmas vacation" is now called "Winter vacation." Even "Merry Christmas" is often replaced with the inoffensive, all-purpose "Happy Holidays."

Savvy merchants have Hanukkah scenes painted on their store windows right next to Santa Claus and stock their aisles with blue and white pre-wrapped Hanukkah gifts right along side the red and green wrapped Christmas presents. Card shops feature Hanukkah sections, albeit tiny ones compared to the Christmas displays. Mall owners place a *hanukkiyah* right next to the Christmas tree.

And, in what must have been a first in American history, the President of the United States played dreidle in a ceremony less than a week after he lit the White House Christmas tree in 1989. Will he light the White House *Hanukkiyah* next year?

Now, it is true that Jews living in a major Jewish population center are more likely to see Hanukkah in the marketplace than Jews living in smaller communities. Yet, it seems that Hanukkah is no longer a holiday to be ignored.

The so-called "Judeo-Christian heritage" has spawned the Christmas-Hanukkah shopping season. Of course, the problem with hyphenated shopping seasons is the same as the problem with hyphenated heritages: the confusion of one with the other.

One of the December Dilemmas is whether Jews should be happy or not with the developing commercialization of Hanukkah. There are those for whom the elevation of Hanukkah is repugnant. It forces comparisons that are difficult to make. It encourages the embellishment of a Jewish holiday for which there is little traditional ritual. Any such attempt is a futile attempt to compete with Christmas, and why should we try to do that when there is no way to win. Let's keep Hanukkah the minor holiday it is, de-emphasizing the decorations, the presents, and the public displays.

Yet, there are others who have concluded, "If you can't beat 'em, join 'em." Luckily Hanukkah comes when it does. At least we have something to celebrate too at a time when it feels as if the whole word is geared to family gatherings, gift exchanges, and good cheer. And besides, these Hanukkah-embellishers argue, have not Jewish holidays always held more or less importance and meaning for Jews depending on when and where they have lived?

Purim, a celebration of the physical survival of the Jews, was a much more popular holiday in places and times where Jews lived under the threat of bodily harm. Hanukkah, a celebration of the spiritual survival of Judaism, is the ideal foil to a Christian holiday which, in its secular formulation, represents the threat of assimilation in our own day.

PSEUDO-CHRISTMAS AND FAMILY GATHERINGS

Adding to the confusion of the season is the fact that Christmas is a legal holiday and the one day of the year when virtually every business and office is closed. For many Jewish families, it is an ideal opportunity for a family gathering. Since nearly every such event has a celebratory nature to it, there is food, drink, conversation, games, and more. In some Jewish families, when they gather on Christmas Day, there is also an exchange of presents, even in those years when Hanukkah comes days or even weeks earlier. There are other Jewish families who go even further, creating a kind of "pseudo-Christmas" by hanging blue and white stockings and constructing a so-called 'Hanukkah bush.'

The temptation for these families to turn the day into a pseudo-Christmas is almost too much to bear. It is so convenient. What difference does it make that Hanukkah was three weeks ago? The important thing is that the entire family can be together and exchange gifts.

Clearly, when Hanukkah and Christmas fall on the same date, there is a much cleaner solution to the problem. In 1989, for example, the third night of Hanukkah fell on Christmas eve. Engaging in a traditional Hanukkah celebration on that night and the following evening presents no problem whatsoever, and everyone feels that they have participated in the season.

But, when Hanukkah falls early in December which, as indicated in the list of dates on the opposite page, will happen two of every three years during the next 60 years, then the solution of simultaneous celebration is unavailable. What is a holiday if not the commemoration of a particular time, of marking that time and making it special? It is entirely inappropriate to "delay" the celebration of the holiday to a "day off," regardless of how convenient that might be. Even a "pseudo-Hanukkah" celebration on December 25 when Hanukkah ended on December 10 is not consistent with Jewish law and custom.

So, what are Jews to do on December 25? Many families do gather together for the day, but simply to enjoy each other's company. Some try to avoid Christmas altogether by leaving town on vacation. A favorite activity is to take advantage of the relatively small numbers of people in the movie theaters and see the latest movie. However, don't be surprised if you find the theater packed with Jewish friends and their families, all of whom had the same idea!

Perhaps the best idea of all is to find a way to enable Christians to fully celebrate Christmas. B'nai B'rith sponsors a program for its members to relieve Christian workers from a wide variety of jobs that must be filled on Christmas, particularly those who work in hospitals and other necessary services. Or, some families might want to volunteer their time to help out at a shelter for the homeless. Certainly, there are meaningful ways to spend this time and demonstrate by your actions a commitment to important Jewish values, even on Christmas Day.

HANUKKAH CALENDAR

Have you ever wondered why the first night of Hanukkah changes each year? It has to do with the fact that the Jewish calendar is based on a unique combination of solar and lunar factors that serve to vary the calendar every year. Some years, Jewish leap years, an extra *month* is added to the calendar which significantly alters the dates of holidays. Unlike the Roman calendar with its fixed dates of holidays (Christmas always falls on December 25), the Jewish festivals fall on the same Jewish date (Hanukkah always falls on 25 Kislev), but the secular date changes yearly.

Since the timing of Hanukkah is so important in dealing with the December Dilemmas, we have researched the dates when Hanukkah falls for the next 60 years. The first date represents the first night of Hanukkah.

Notice that Hanukkah and Christmas fall together only eighteen times in the sixty years between 1990-2050.

5751—1990—December 11-18	5782—2021—November 28-December 5
5752—1991—December 1-8	5783—2022—December 18-25
5753—1992—December 19-26	5784—2023—December 7-14
5754—1993—December 8-15	5785—2024—December 25-January 1
5755—1994—November 27-December 4	5786—2025—December 14-21
5756—1995—December 17-24	5787—2026—December 4-11
5757—1996—December 5-12	5788—2027—December 24-31
5758—1997—December 23-30	5789—2028—December 12-19
5759—1998—December 13-20	5790—2029—December 1-8
5760—1999—December 3-10	5791—2030—December 20-27
5761—2000—December 22-29	5792—2031—December 9-16
5762—2001—December 9-16	5793—2032—November 27-December 4
5763—2002—November 29-December 6	5794—2033—December 16-23
5764—2003—December 19-26	5795—2034—December 6-13
5765—2004—December 7-14	5796—2035—December 25-January 1
5766—2005—December 25-January 1	5797—2036—December 13-20
5767—2006—December 15-22	5798—2037—December 2-9
5768—2007—December 4-11	5799—2038—December 21-28
5769—2008—December 21-28	5800—2039—December 11-18
5770—2009—December 11-18	5801—2040—November 29-December 6
5771—2010—December 1-8	5802—2041—December 17-24
5772—2011—December 20-27	5803—2042—December 7-14
5773—2012—December 8-15	5804—2043—December 26-January 2
5774—2013—November 27-December 4	5805—2044—December 14-21
5775—2014—December 16-23	5806—2045—December 3-10
5776—2015—December 6-13	5807—2046—December 23-30
5777—2016—December 24-31	5808—2047—December 12-19
5778—2017—December 12-19	5809—2048—November 29-December 6
5779—2018—December 2-9	5810—2049—December 19-26
5780—2019—December 22-29	5811—2050—December 9-16
5781—2020—December 10-17	

JEWS-BY-CHOICE AND CHRISTMAS

One of the most profound changes in Jewish family life during the past forty years has been the significant rate of intermarriage between Jew and Gentile. Whatever the particular percentage of first marriages cited as intermarriages in any year (estimates range from 25%–50% and higher), the undeniable fact is that one of the consequences of intermarriage is that it introduces into the family a person who was not born Jewish.

This not-born-Jewish person brings with him/her a history of associations, memories, and emotions about the winter holidays, usually about Christmas. And, whatever path the person chooses—whether s/he converts to Judaism or doesn't—the pull of Christmas is powerful indeed.

In fact, intermarriage experts agree that how a couple negotiates the Christmas-Hanukkah season often becomes the true test of the viability of an intermarriage.

It is a complicated problem. Most born Christians equate Christmas with the warmest memories of family, special times, beautiful decorations, gift-giving, and more. Even for those who are not particularly religious, Christmas, and especially the Christmas tree, has a special attraction.

The Jewish partner in an intermarriage often has feelings about Christmas as well, and they are usually not pleasant. For many Jews, Christmas was a time of feeling left-out, jealous, anxious—at best, ambivalent. The tree symbolizes the struggle to maintain a Jewish identity in the majority culture.

With these two diametrically opposed sets of feelings, the battle for the religious identity of an intermarriage is often fought in the shadow of the Christmas tree.

We want to explore the issues facing the entire family when an intermarriage occurs. And, although we will see that there are differences in approaching the problem depending on the status of the not-born-Jewish person, the repercussions ripple throughout the family system.

One key distinction is whether or not the not-born-Jewish person has converted. When a Gentile becomes a Jew-by-Choice, s/he totally accepts Judaism and is accepted as a Jew into the community. One would expect that through the conversion process, the issues raised by Christmas would be worked through. According to many professionals who work with converts, this is much easier said than done.

In fact, often the most difficult part of converting to Judaism is to let go of the Christmas holiday. Imagine a Jew being asked to give up the Passover Seder or the High Holidays. Some converts can do so relatively easily, for they are embracing a religion brimming with holidays and life cycle celebrations. Others cannot abandon Christmas so quickly, experiencing a profound sense of loss personally, facing the possiblity of being cut off from one's family, and losing the opportunity as a parent to share this holiday with children.

For the Jewish partner, there are serious problems as well. If the couple celebrates Christmas, the Jew may feel guilty, alienated from his family, and fearful that his/her children will never achieve a sense of Jewish identity.

Thus, one of the most important decisions to be made when a Jew and Gentile marry is what to do about the winter holidays. Some couples decide before they are married that one religion will be observed in the family. This would be expected if the Gentile converted to Judaism. Mixed-marrieds, wherein the Gentile does not convert, often try to incorporate both Christmas and Hanukkah into their winter celebration.

The "both holiday" solution faces its most difficult test when children are born. Most experts agree that children raised in two religious traditions often end up like Benjamin Disraeli who, when asked what religion he was, answered that he was like the page separating the Old and New Testaments, **blank**. They recommend that intermarried parents choose one religion to teach children and celebrate its holidays fully. Judy Personk and Jim Remsen in *The Intermarriage Handbook* caution:

> "We think that people who say they are raising their children Jewish, but have a tree and celebrate Christmas, are in effect not raising them in one religion. In America, the tree is such a potent symbol that it alone introduces the second religion into the home. If you have a tree, you have as much Christianity in your home as many Christian families..."

Their recommendation:

> "Celebrate Hanukkah enthusiastically and have your Jewish life throughout the year be vibrant enough to outshine Christmas's once-a-year dazzle..."

Assuming the couple takes this advice, raises their children Jewish, celebrating only Hanukkah in the home, there is one complicating factor that cannot be dismissed by this decision:

The family of origin of a Jew-by-Choice does not convert.

This is an extremely important point and raises one of the most challenging obstacles to resolving this particular December Dilemma: What do I do about celebrating Christmas and Hanukkah with my family when my family includes both Jews and Christians? What can I do when Christian relatives invite my family for Christmas?

Before we suggest some options, it is important to understand how difficult, if not impossible, and perhaps undesirable it would be to ignore the fact that non-Jewish grandparents cannot be expected to give up their holiday just because one of their children converted out of their religion. As grandparents, they will more than likely expect their now-Jewish child to respect their religion and their right to share their holidays with their grandchildren.

To complicate matters, the parents of the born Jew in the couple may be frantic about the possibility that their grandchildren might "celebrate" Christmas with their Christian counterparts. And, in most family systems, they are likely to let their fears be known.

All this puts the Jew-by-Choice and his/her spouse in a very difficult position. After talking to many intermarried couples and surveying the current (and growing) literature on the subject, here are some of the choices available, ranging from total avoidance to reasoned compromise:

1.   Go out of town for the holidays.

2.   Do not recognize their holiday at all. Celebrate Thanksgiving, Fourth of July, Memorial Day—any non-religious holiday—with them.

3.   Do not accept an invitation for Christmas. Send or bring gifts to the grandparents at another time.

4.   Ask the non-Jewish grandparents to celebrate Hanukkah with you when Hanukkah occurs—not on December 25.

5.   Go to the Christian grandparents for Christmas, but make it very clear that "this is Grandpa and Grandma's holiday, not ours. Nevertheless, we can enjoy sharing it with them." Just as Jewish parents or grandparents might invite Christian in-laws to a Passover Seder, "sharing" a religious holiday other than our own is quite different than "observing" it in our own home.

KOSHER TURKEY FOR CHRISTMAS DINNER?

Many of the people we consulted about this issue, including rabbis, educators, and family psychologists, agree that it is possible for children to distinguish between "their" holidays and "others'" holidays, even when the "others" are as significant as grandparents. And, if it is true, as anecdotal evidence seems to indicate, that many intermarried families do "share" Christmas with the Christian members of their extended families, then some very interesting wrinkles to the problem emerge.

For example, what shall we do about gift exchanges? We want Jewish children to receive Hanukkah gifts during Hanukkah, while non-Jewish relatives will certainly expect Christmas presents on Christmas. The same is true for greetings cards.

Now, it will seem strange at first for non-Jews to seek out Hanukkah cards, to wrap gifts with Hanukkah wrapping, and to become sensitive to the fact that Hanukkah may occur weeks before Christmas. And, in what is certainly one of the great ironies of this particular December Dilemma, we may find a rather large percentage of the Jewish community shopping for Christmas presents for Christian relatives in the family!

Lydia Kukoff, a Jew-by-Choice and the Director of Outreach for the Union of American Hebrew Congregations, reports that while she gives all of her non-Jewish relatives Christmas presents, it is very difficult for her mother not to give her Jewish grandchildren gifts wrapped for Christmas. Lydia's children understand that this makes Grandma feel good and they are certainly not confused about which holiday is theirs. Lydia explains: "If I told my mother to give the kids Hanukkah presents, it would be like rubbing salt into an open wound." Just as she feels it is important to clearly establish the Jewishness of one's home, Lydia implores people to take an empathetic view from the perspective of the non-Jewish relative. "After all," she says, "everytime my mother visits me, she has to deal with the rules of a kosher kitchen!"

It can get even more complicated. Consider the following scenario: You are married to a Jew-by-Choice. You and your spouse have created a warm, vibrant Jewish home, fully observant of Jewish holidays and Jewish law, including *kashrut* (the Jewish dietary code). Your Christian in-laws invite you and your family for Christmas dinner. You agree to attend.

Will they serve you kosher turkey?

Take it a step further. Let's say that this particular year, the third night of Hanukkah coincides with Christmas eve.

Will you pack up your *hanukkiyah* and light candles alongside the Christmas tree?

SOLVING THE DECEMBER DILEMMAS

It is impossible to offer clear and easy solutions to the December Dilemmas. Yet, everything we have discussed reduces to one object: the need to create guidelines and draw borders around one's religious practices.

Where do you draw the line?

Will you let your children watch Christmas television shows, but not sit on Santa's knee in the mall?

Will you take the family to see the Christmas decorations in the neighborhood, but not participate in the public lighting of a *hanukkiyah*?

Will you go to Christmas dinner?

Will you embellish Hanukkah into a major celebration or leave it as a minor holiday in your home?

Whatever the dilemma, the place to begin is with yourself. Explore your own feelings about the dilemma. Clarify for yourself your position, list the arguments that defend it. Then, if you are married, begin a dialogue with your spouse. Be open to his/her feelings and opinions. Try to reach an agreement about a plan of action. If you have children, explain your decision to them. This is an incredible opportunity to share with them your feelings, beliefs, and a good deal of information about the holidays.

If the dilemma you are facing involves negotiating the celebration of holidays with Christian relatives, the most important advice to all parties involved is to try to work out a plan for handling the holidays *in July*, not the day you get an invitation for Christmas dinner. The holiday season is loaded with emotional overtones. The discussions could very well generate powerful feelings of pain, guilt, betrayal and rejection, just to mention a few. The debate about holiday celebration in the family can easily become a smoke screen for unspoken feelings about the intermarriage, how children and grandchildren are being raised, and the rights of parents and grandparents. When taken out of the immediate context of the holidays themselves, the voice of rationality and relatively dispassionate discourse might be heard.

When your position is clarified, visit your parents, in-laws, and/or other relatives (in person and in July, if possible) to discuss your position about the December holidays. Share with them how *you* understand the meaning of the holidays, especially if it is different than the way they view them. Be very specific about what you want done. If you want your Christian relatives to send your children presents wrapped in Hanukkah paper, say so. If you are willing to visit non-Jewish grandparents to trim a Christmas tree, but not on Christmas itself, say so. If you have decided to accept an invitation for Christmas Day, but will not accompany the family to church, say so. Listen sympathetically to other positions, especially to the feelings your decision generates in others, but stand your ground. Be consistent and others will respect you. Yet, be aware and open to new information, new suggestions, and new realities the next time around.

Another important understanding: The solutions to the December Dilemmas are likely to be worked out *over a period of years*, not all at once and forever. It takes time for people to change their thinking about deeply-held positions and desires. It will take time for relatives to understand your position. It may take some experimentation with modes of celebration to find a workable strategy. Decisions may also change as children grow from childhood to adolescence. Above all, try to avoid confrontation—muster all the patience, compassion, and understanding you can.

The bottom line may be that Jewish families with non-Jewish relatives have to find ways to coexist—throughout the year, but particularly during the season of the December Dilemmas. And, as we have seen, Jewish parents often must find ways to cope with what Rabbi Harold Schulweis calls "the Santa Claustrophobia" of the season.

Finally, seek out others with whom to share your concerns and experiences. Many synagogues and religious schools offer workshops on dealing with the December Dilemmas. Attend them, share your story, listen to the stories of others. There may be a rabbi, a Jewish educator, or even a psychologist available to help you through the issues.

In addition to the ideas and potential solutions you may hear, there is a sense of relief knowing that you are not alone in facing these problems.

The December Dilemmas will be with us for a long time to come. They can prove difficult to solve. Yet, they can also provide an opportunity to clarify one's Jewish identity, to establish the Jewish identity of one's family, and to assert one's commitment to Judaism and the Jewish people in the face of pressures to assimilate into the majority culture. Is this not the same challenge the Maccabees confronted? Is this not a lesson of the Hanukkah story? Is this not one of the most important goals of our celebration of Hanukkah today?

In a way, it would be much easier if Hanukkah came in July. But, in a strange twist of irony, the proximity of Hanukkah to Christmas does force a fundamental definition of who we are. If Hanukkah encourages us to publicly and proudly affirm our Jewish identities, then perhaps it deserves to be the major holiday it most assuredly has become.

AFTERWORD

WHAT IS HANUKKAH?

Ultimately, we are back again at the question which began this book:

What is Hanukkah?

What we have learned over the course of creating these pages is that Hanukkah is an ever-evolving process. It includes practices that conjure stories which are constantly retold in ways that stretch ancient values to meet contemporary meanings. Hanukkah has its own meanings—and it has many, as yet unrevealed, meanings which will come clear only as we are obligated to create the next retelling.

The ritual of lighting the *hanukkiyah* is an act of publicizing one's Jewish belief in the miracles which God can work, in the constant availability of hope. As each generation passes this ancient custom on, parents are constantly teaching their children that the battle can be won, that darkness can be overcome, that inspired and enlightened by God's teachings, almost anything is possible. As difficult as the winter season may be, as confusing as its problems may seem, Hanukkah stands as a symbol of the possible. Its simple acts—lighting, blessing, and telling— give us tools to constantly work miracles. That is but one of the gifts which comes from living Jewish life artfully.

SELECTED BIBLIOGRAPHY

ELKE: Tell Ron the story we read about that girl Dena. You know, how her grandfather helped her make her *ḥanukkiyah* so that she could light it herself. They made it out of what, remember?

ORLY: Potatoes. They put the candles in a half of a potato. That way she could light the other candles without burning herself. She did not have a *ḥanukkiyah*, but her brothers and sisters did and she felt left out. Her *saba* or *zadie* helped her make a special one.

RESOURCE BOOKS

Elias Bickerman, *From Ezra to the Last of the Maccabees*. Schocken Books, New York, 1949.
    One of the best historical accounts of Hanukkah.

Paul Cowan and Rachel Cowan, *Mixed Blessings*. Doubleday, New York, 1987.
    Excellent suggestions for intermarrieds coping with the winter season.

Elysse D. Frishman and Leonard Baskin, *Haneirot Halalu—These Lights are Holy: A Home Celebration of Chanuka*. Central Conference of Reform Rabbis Press, New York, 1989.
    A family liturgy for Hanukkah, illustrated beautifully by Leonard Baskin.

Philip Goodman, *The Hanukkah Anthology*. Jewish Publication Society, Philadelphia, 1976.
    Comprehensive collection of Hanukkah information.

Blu Greenberg, *How To Run A Traditional Jewish Household*. Simon and Schuster, New York, 1983.
    See the chapter on Hanukkah for a modern Orthodox approach to celebrating the holiday.

Irving Greenberg, *The Jewish Way: Living the Holidays*. Summit Books, New York, 1988.
    Superb chapter on Hanukkah by one of our leading teachers.

Lydia Kukoff, *Choosing Judaism*. Union of American Hebrew Congregations, New York, 1981.
    Basic guide to Judaism for Jews-by-Choice.

Harold Kushner, *When Children Ask About God*. Reconstructionist Press, New York, 1971.
    See chapter on miracles.

Judy Personk and Jim Remsen, *The Intermarriage Handbook: A Guide for Jews and Christians*. Arbor House, New York, 1988.
    Sensitive suggestions for intermarrieds on handling the December Dilemmas.

Mae Shafter Rockland, *The Hanukkah Book*. Schocken Books, New York, 1977.
    Excellent compilation of Hanukkah celebration ideas and crafts.

Michael Strassfeld, *The Jewish Holidays*. Harper and Row, New York, 1985.
    Fine chapter on Hanukkah.

CHILDREN'S LITERATURE

David A. Adler, *A Picture Book of Hanukkah*. Holiday House, New York, 1982.
    Fine introduction to Hanukkah for young children.

Jane Berman, *The Eight Nights: A Chanukah Counting Book*. Union of American Hebrew Congregations, New York, 1978.
    A first book for Hanukkah. Pre-school.

Chaya Burstein, *Hanukkah Cat*. Kar Ben Copies, Inc., Rockville, MD, 1985.
    Cute cat causes Hanukkah conundrums.

Miriam Chaikin, *Light Another Candle*. Clarion Books, New York, 1981.
    The Hanukkah story and celebration.

Barbara Cohen, *The Christmas Revolution*, Lothrop, Lee and Shepard Books, New York, 1987.
    Emily, a fourth grader, must think about her own Jewish heritage when a new boy, an Orthodox Jew, refuses to participate in the school's Christmas pageant.

Malka Drucker, *Hanukkah: Eight Nights, Eight Lights*. Holiday House, New York, 1980.
    An excellent book featuring the historical account of Hanukkah and creative ideas for celebration. Middle grades.

Marilyn Hirsh, *Potato Pancakes All Around: A Hanukkah Tale*. Jewish Publication Society, Philadelphia, 1982.
    Cleverly illustrated Hanukkah fable about a town's experience with latkes.

Joel Lurie Grishaver, *Building Jewish Life: Hanukkah*. Torah Aura Productions, 4423 Fruitland Avenue, Los Angeles, CA, 90058, 1987.
    A superb introduction to Hanukkah, written for 7-10 year olds and their parents, featuring a favorite story entitled "The Return of the Junkyard Menorah or How Judi Learned That It's Important to be Different."

Vicky Kelman, *Together: A Child-Parent Kit—Hanukkah*, Melton Research Center, New York, 1984.
    Wonderful information and activities for parents and children to share together. For 7-9 year olds and their parents.

Eric Kimmel, *Herschel and the Hanukkah Goblins*. Holiday House, New York, 1985.
    Spooky tale of Hanukkah. Wonderful illustrations.

Deborah Uchill Miller and Karen Ostrove, *Modi'in Motel: An Idol Tale for Chanukah*. Kar-Ben Copies, Inc., Rockville, MD, 1986.
Another delightful "Dr. Seuss"-type book from the folks who brought you *Only Nine Chairs*.

Judith Saypol and Madeline Wikler, *My Very Own Chanukah*, Kar-Ben Copies, Inc, Rockville, MD, 1978.
A preschool introduction to the holiday.

Elleen Sherman, *The Odd Potato: A Chanukah Story*. Kar Ben Copies, Inc., Rockville, MD, 1984.
Based on a popular nursery school craft project—the potato menorah.

Isaac Bashevis Singer, *The Power of Light*. Farrar, Straus and Giroux, New York, 1980.
A wonderful collection of stories by the master storyteller.

Susan Sussman, *There Is No Such Thing as a Chanukah Bush, Sandy Goldstein*, Albert Whitman & Co., Niles, Illinois, 1983.
Robin is confused when her Jewish friend, Sandy Goldstein, is allowed to have a Christmas tree and Robin cannot. Her wise grandfather helps Robin cope with the dilemma.

Sadie Rose Weilerstein, *K'tonton in the Circus, A Hanukkah Adventure*. Jewish Publication Society, Philadelphia, 1981.
Another tale of the Jewish "Tom Thumb" at Hanukkah time. A good read-aloud for families with young children.

Jeffrey S. Winter, *A Hanukkah Letter from Moscow*. Contemporary Designs, P.O.B. 60, 213 Main Street, Gilbert, Iowa, 50105, 1990.
Contemporary story about Soviet Jews and their struggle for religious freedom.

Yehuda and Sara Wurtzel, *Lights: A Fable About Hanukkah*. Gesher/Jerusalem Productions, Rossel Books, Chappaqua, NY, 1984.
A volume based on the popular videotape.

Jane Breskin Zalben, *Beni's First Chanukah*. Henry Holt and Company, New York, 1988.
A family of bears enjoys candles, latkes, and a visit from some non-Jewish bears. For very young children.

MAGAZINE ARTICLES

"Christmas and Hanukkah in the Public Schools: One Community's Dilemma." B. Firestone. Jewish Education 37:180-7, #4, 1967.

"Christmas and Hanukkah." M. Harris, Jewish Digest 26:32-6, December 1980.

"A Midrash for Hanukkah." Bernard H. Mehlman and Daniel F. Polish, Conservative Judaism, 36, Issue 2, Winter, 1982.

"The December Dilemma." Mae Shafter Rockland. Hadassah Magazine, 67:21-3 December, 1985.

"Alienation: Christmas comes to a Jewish Home." Ann Roiphe. Moment 4:18-19, January-February, 1979.

"A Meditation on *Maoz Zur.*" Ismar Schorsch, Judaism, 37:459-464, Issue 148, Fall, 1988.

VIDEOTAPES

"Benjamin and the Miracle of Hanukkah," Ergo Media, POB 2037, Teaneck, NJ, 07666.
   Young Benjamin is chosen by Judah the Maccabee to bring holy oil to Jerusalem. Wonderful narration by Herschel Bernardi, fair animation, lovely music, and an unfortunate mistake—the Temple Menorah had seven branches, not nine.

"A Hanukkah Celebration," Ergo Media, POB 2037, Teaneck, NJ, 07666.
   Nice compilation of puppet plays, a visit to Modi'in, and how to make *sufganiyot.*

"The Animated Menorah," Scopus Films, POB 21372, Woodhaven, NY 11421.
   Claymation stories by the same folks who produced "The Animated Haggadah."

AUDIOTAPES

"Chanukah: A Singing Celebration with Cindy Paley," Cindy Paley Aboudy, 14246 Chandler Boulevard, Van Nuys, CA, 91401.
   Excellent collection of popular Hanukkah songs by an easy-to-follow singer.

"Stories of Hanukkah," told by Cherie Karo Schwartz, Kar Ben Copies, Inc., Rockville, MD.
   "Hanukkah Cat," "The Odd Potato," and "Nathan's Hanukkah Bargain" are read aloud.